Breaking Free from Critical Addiction

Our #1 Social Disease

Kalie Marino

Edited by: Pamela Maliniak

BALBOA.
PRESS
A DIVISION OF HAY HOUSE

ISBN: 978-1-4525-5484-6 (sc)
ISBN: 978-1-4525-5485-3 (hc)
ISNB: 978-1-4525-5483-9 (e)

Library of Congress Control Number: 2012913886

Balboa Press books may be ordered through booksellers or by contacting:

Balboa Press
A Division of Hay House
1663 Liberty Drive
Bloomington, IN 47403
www.balboapress.com
1-(877) 407-4847

Because of the dynamic nature of the Internet, any web addresses or links contained in this book may have changed since publication and may no longer be valid. The views expressed in this work are solely those of the author and do not necessarily reflect the views of the publisher, and the publisher hereby disclaims any responsibility for them.

The author of this book does not dispense medical advice or prescribe the use of any technique as a form of treatment for physical, emotional, or medical problems without the advice of a physician, either directly or indirectly. The intent of the author is only to offer information of a general nature to help you in your quest for emotional and spiritual well-being. In the event you use any of the information in this book for yourself, which is your constitutional right, the author and the publisher assume no responsibility for your actions.

Any people depicted in stock imagery provided by Thinkstock are models, and such images are being used for illustrative purposes only. Certain stock imagery © Thinkstock.

Printed in the United States of America

Balboa Press rev. date: 8/20/2012

In memory of our son, Michael Marino, Jr., who was killed as this went to press. The circumstances of his death point out the importance of identifying and treating critical addiction.

To my husband, Michael, my best friend, partner, playmate, lover, muse, and healer ... the most unconditionally loving person I know. Thank you for your support.

With gratitude to my friends, Kathleen Bartuneck and Kevin Bidner, for their supportive suggestions; to my son, Angel, for making sure I finished this book; to my son, David Cook, for creating and maintaining my websites; and to Pamela Maliniak for her insightful and creative editing. Working with her was like having a writing partner.

Contents

Foreword

Breaking Free from Critical Addiction shines a glaring light on one of the greatest challenges of our era. It takes the position that criticism and other forms of negativity are rampant in our culture, containing within it seeds of both individual and global destruction. With the ability to reframe "What's wrong with this picture?" to "What could be right about it?", Kalie Marino has been able to simplify a massive topic into one which anyone can explore and find value.

I have known Kalie Marino for more than two decades, and in that time, I have found her to be a woman of integrity, insight, and wisdom. As an ordained interfaith minister and master's level clinical social worker, Kalie approaches this epidemic from both perspectives—the psychological and the spiritual. The toll that criticism takes on our sense of self-worth and our relationships is immeasurable. Also immeasurable is the benefit of discovering ways in which to ward it off, transmuting destructive patterns such as anger, depression, disease, and addiction into brightly shining, paradigm shifting concepts like peace, truth, and raising our vibration.

The book is broken down into easily digestible concepts, beginning with defining criticism and other forms of negativity as a serious social problem and then exploring its origins, impact, and examples of ways in which it insidiously eats away at the foundation of our sense of self and society. It then carries us forward into remedies, including the timeless Golden Rule, which is a hallmark of all faith traditions.

A consummate story teller, Kalie weaves fascinating tales from her own life and those of her clients, family, and friends as examples of the destructive nature of critical addiction, as well as the healing power of understanding, forgiveness, and compassion. Humor permeates the pages; my favorite story shows up near the final pages as Kalie finds a creative way to solve the problem of a damaged water heater, while remaining in integrity with her highest values. It had me knowingly laughing.

It is no surprise that I am being called upon to write this foreword, since I have my very own impish—and sometimes obnoxiously active— chattering, monkey mind Inner Critic who delights in pointing out my shortcomings. Furthermore, Kalie and I have much in common, including our educational background and career path. I too am an MSW and interfaith minister who graduated from The New Seminary.

I find *Breaking Free from Critical Addiction* to be an invaluable guide for living an authentic life. I would love to see this book on the reading list of institutions that educate those in the helping professionals; I can only imagine how many more people we might have helped in being exposed to these concepts in our training. The good news is that it's now available for professionals and lay people alike.

As you read these pages, may you discover the beauty and brilliance of the one who gazes back at you in your mirror. I wish you that blissing and blessing, as well as much enlightenment and learning on your path in this book and beyond.

Reverend Edie Weinstein, MSW, LSW, is journalist, motivational speaker, interfaith minister, bliss coach, clinical social worker, and author of *The Bliss Mistress Guide To Transforming the Ordinary Into the Extraordinary*. Learn more at www.liveinjoy.org.

Prologue

When I first entered the master's program for clinical social work, we were told that social workers are change agents. This title excited me. I thought a change agent must be an expert in the change process—a mechanic to the soul—one who knew exactly what to do in order to bring about healing and happiness. So I asked, "What's change?"

Sorely disappointed, I discovered that these expert change agents didn't have an answer, but I was excited for the challenge of discovering it for myself. Thus began my search to understand how the mind works and how we make significant changes.

I learned that there are two kinds of change. The first is the simple kind of change, like rearranging your furniture. This happens frequently and fairly effortlessly. The second kind of change is transformational and involves a change in identity. It is like turning a garage into a recreation room … same place but with a different identity. I wanted to know how to bring about these big, transformational changes in people's lives.

I have a background in quantum physics theory, which is a science that gives insight into the effect consciousness has on the world and change itself. I included quantum theory in my master's thesis and called it: "An Heuristic View of Change, Integrating Time, Consciousness and Energy." It took an inquiring view at discovering how transformation happens and how to create significant change.

The experiment I designed in my research demonstrated that a person's state of mind can cause significant physical effects. This discovery made headlines in *The Brain/Mind Bulletin*, a national scientific publication, and my experiment was reproduced around the world with the same repeatable results. This research was merely the beginning of an exciting adventure in consciousness.

Fascinated by what I call the mechanics of the mind and how the mind works, I have continued to study the mind and experiment with various ways to create perceptual shifts in understanding. I offer my clients insights and tools that empower them to discover their strengths and Authentic Selves. I *have* become a change agent—one who is still growing, still learning, and constantly witnessing miracles in my office as people shift perception and transform before my eyes, each one inspiring me and teaching me something new.

Most people do not know how the mind works. Many have heard that we create our own reality, but I have found very few people who actually understand how to do that. And while creating what you want is not the focus of this book, we are laying the foundation necessary by first undoing any negativity that stands in your way. You might say that this book is a mental detox for cleansing the mind in preparation for creating your heart's desire. Strength, happiness, and your Authentic Self will begin to emerge as a side effect of this cleansing. We will focus on conscious creation in the next book.

If those around us have to change for us to 'be okay', we are held hostage by those who impact our lives the most. Then there is no hope for making real changes in our lives. However, when we realize that the problem is within our own minds, we are free to change it, and transformation in our life becomes possible. Making this realization concrete gives people a more resilient center, enabling them to make it through anything. Freedom from criticism and negativity is the gift that I offer to you, my readers, but you can only receive it by applying the Four Steps to Freedom directly in your life.

My goal is to write about transformation in a way that is easy to read and can help anyone feel safe enough to examine their own critical thinking, because the first lesson is that we are all innocent, even when we are critical. We did not cause this problem, but we are the only ones who can change it. As you examine the way we think and discover where we got our false assumptions, you will naturally begin to question these assumptions, and they will crumble. You will see how you can transform your thinking, discover your strengths, and create happier lives for yourself and others.

There is an old Chinese folktale about a group of blind men trying to describe an elephant. Each one can only feel one part of the elephant, so they all come to different conclusions. The one who holds the tail thinks the elephant is like a rope, while another blind man feels two legs and says an elephant is like trunks of trees that have no leaves. The one touching the belly thinks it is a huge wall, and the one holding its ear thinks it is a large fan. Touching the tusk, yet another blind man thinks the elephant is a hard pipe.

We look at social problems like we are blind men looking at an elephant. We each only see one small part of the problem and not what connects them. Problems like poverty, disease, conflict, unemployment, terrorism, drugs, and social unrest do not happen in isolation. They are all aspects of one social problem, and we are blind to the energetic and emotional body that connects them.

The blind men and the elephant is the analytical paradigm that has us looking at parts instead of the whole. Analysts struggle each day to make sense of social and economic data, stumbling blindly, touching only small parts of the information, and coming away with a narrow and fragmented understanding of what it means. This is like the doctor who dissects a dead body piece by piece to learn about life. To learn about life, we need to look at a bigger picture of what we have in common in order to pinpoint what is truly creating our problems.

The last thing deep-water fish discover is water, even though it is all around them. Fish notice what is in the water, but not the water itself. They may never discover water unless they jump out of it. That is how Einstein made his profound discoveries. He was a meditator. He left the world and went into the spheres for new knowledge. He said he got all of his insights from the universe, a perspective beyond his social conditioning and scientific beliefs. He looked at problems from a meta-perspective beyond the problems.

Since our social conditioning and scientific beliefs limit what we see, I invite you to join me on a trip into inner space for a meta-perspective on our inner world—the world behind the eyes. Let's see what we have in common within us that could be causing our social problems. By eliminating what separates us, we may discover new strengths and creative qualities that emerge through experiencing our connection with each other.

Our journey begins by seeing the underlying similarity in faultfinding and negativity that pervades the thinking of our society. Next, we begin to focus inward on the Inner Critic that taunts us, creating negativity—followed by noticing the types of coping strategies people develop as attempts to get rid of it. The cover of this book is symbolic of that inner struggle for freedom from inner tyranny. After we explore the Critic's origins, we focus on how to cleanse our inner world naturally and spontaneously. You will enjoy fresh insights and develop new coping strategies that create happiness instead of negativity.

I do hope you enjoy the journey. I am your tour guide and will accompany you along the way, furnishing you with understanding and tools to make it all the more pleasant. If you have questions, please feel free to contact me through my website at CriticalAddiction.com. We are instituting this new website so that you can post your experiences in applying the principles contained within this book, as well as ask questions. It is my prayer that we take this journey together and make a difference in the world.

Enjoy!

Kalie

PART I:
IDENTIFYING THE PROBLEM

What Is Critical Addiction?

**Some people look at a glass and see it as half full,
while critics look at the same glass
and see it as almost empty.**

Our society has become addicted to criticism and other forms of negativity, which is a social disease of epidemic proportion that goes unnoticed as a silent killer of both life and happiness. The news media focuses on disasters and bad news, because good news does not sell nearly as well as the bad. From true-life horrors to anticipated natural disasters (and everything in between), movies filled with violence and impending doom do quite well at the box office.

We live in an atmosphere of fear and doubt, one in which everything and everyone is scrutinized and judged. Even small children are under pressure to compete and perform as never before. Spouses find fault with each other, and the divorce rate climbs. Many carry grievances that perpetuate cycles of attack and vengeance, reviving old conflicts and creating new conflicts—even wars.

The emotional stresses of society are seen in the rise of addictions of all kinds. As anxiety and stress grow, illness and disease becomes more prevalent, because criticism and negativity wear on the body and weaken the immune system. Viruses mutate and multiply as their underlying emotional cause goes unnoticed and untreated. This hidden addiction is a social disease that is fueling the fire of spiraling emotional, physical, and social problems.

Political campaigns are fought and won with negative ads that criticize opponents or try to ruin their reputation. Politicians talk about what they stand against instead of what they stand for. Our national campaigns are focused on resisting evil. Even though we are fighting a war on poverty, a war on drugs, and a war on terrorism, we are not winning any of them. In fact, the things we are fighting against are growing. Something is wrong.

What happened to <u>resist not evil</u>[1], the advice we were offered in the Christian Bible? Instead of constantly fighting against what we don't want, what has happened to fighting for that which we value ... like our forefathers did when they declared our independence from Great Britain and identified our human rights?

It is time to shine the light on our society's critical approach to life and reevaluate if the approach is in fact working to bring us desirable results. There is overwhelming evidence that criticism is a destructive force. Is this is how we want to live our lives? Is there another way to live? Are we willing to change?

In the next chapter, I show why habitual criticism alone qualifies as a dangerous addiction. In the third chapter, I give examples of how this pervasive negative attitude has become a part of our everyday life, and I list symptoms of critical addiction. Part two of this book focuses on solutions and treatment plans. Part three offers Four Steps to Freedom, while part four explores the energy of consciousness—a new paradigm for understanding behavior that enables us to make major changes or shifts in consciousness more quickly and more easily.

Tragically, most people are unaware of the impact of criticism and negativity on society and themselves. If they are aware, they simply go along with it because everybody's doing it, and they feel helpless to change it. By publicly acknowledging the personal and social problems caused by this judgmental pattern, and by working together for a positive future, we can take steps to make changes that will be rewarding for everyone.

Criticism, while only one aspect of negativity and pessimism, is symbolic of the problem as a whole. It is a mental and emotional process—one of faultfinding in seeking out what is wrong or lacking in each situation, instead of simply noticing what is present and its effects, and then proceeding to choose what we want to come of it.

---

1   Matthew 5:39, *New American Standard Bible*

Criticism can be done with harsh words, name-calling, sarcasm, a put-down, a frown, a sigh of disgust, or a disdainful glance. Worrying about a person making mistakes instead of having faith in them is a covert way of criticizing. Many people realize they worry a lot, but they may not recognize that they are using this anxiety to criticize through various ways. Instead, they may feel virtuous about worrying. Notice here that criticism is a little like dreaming; everybody does it, but not everyone is aware of doing it. Some people criticize out of habit, while others just seem to enjoy doing it. Pessimists are critical and often act superior because they notice possible problems, but research shows that optimists live longer.

Most doctors recognize negative thinking as a contributor to disease, and some doctors go so far as to say that negative thinking is the number one cause of all disease. As a therapist, I have seen clients go into remission once they resolve related emotional issues. If there truly is a relationship between emotional health and disease, our society's critical approach to life has created a social disease that rests at the heart of many maladies plaguing our world.

Educators point out the importance of rewarding positive behavior and showing children the natural consequences of negative behavior. The same thing is true in the workplace. A negative or critical atmosphere lowers productivity and increases costs. Criticism is destructive to self-esteem, toxic to self-confidence, and hinders team building. It simply does not work at any level of our society.

Identifying and changing this addiction is crucial to our survival and wellbeing. While a negative perspective on life is only an attitude, it is itself a critical addiction. Attitude and perspective make the difference between whether we are happy or sad, productive or unproductive, healthy or ailing, and at peace or in conflict in all areas of life. Understanding critical addiction is absolutely necessary to successfully treat all addictions and most of our social problems.

Criticism is mistakenly seen as normal, expected, and even desired as necessary. Most people today are unaware of the negative impact their own criticism has on others and on themselves. Doctors once endorsed cigarettes as good for you, until their destructive and addictive qualities were proven. Behavior that is clearly co-dependent, or symptomatic of love addiction, was once romanticized and glorified in the movies as the way life 'should be', until its destructiveness was identified. The process of habitual criticism, worry, and negativity must also be understood and named for what it is—a destructive addiction and social disease. Once identified and named, recovery is possible.

I wrote this book for the purpose of identifying and naming this insidious addiction and social disease. I wrestled with names, deciding that "critical addiction" best described it. My insightful editor suggested I would do the work of future researchers justice by outlining a specific definition. The best I can do at this time on such a broad term with so many implications is as follows:

Critical addiction is a broad term for problems with habitual negative and critical thinking to the detriment of the addict's self-esteem, relationships, and/or health, causing either low or aggrandized self-esteem, anxiety, anger, depression, paranoia, self-absorption, defeatism, pessimism, and/or feelings of overwhelm, often leading to other forms of addiction of which critical addiction is the primary addiction. Addicts have a compelling attraction to negativity that expresses itself through anger, guilt, and fear, as well as faultfinding of self and others. Critical addiction is spread through social contacts, making it a social disease of immense proportions.

Criticism Destroys Relationships

Your best friend is the one who appreciates you the most. We defend ourselves from critics. So when people carry the habit of criticism into their 'love life', they do not have a love life anymore. They find themselves living with the enemy or divorcing them. As society becomes more critical, the divorce rate rises.

Criticism is experienced as an attack, because it is not based on respect for who we are at our core. When we are criticized, we feel attacked and defend ourselves in one of several ways. We may attack back by finding fault with our attacker, we may comply in an attempt to ward off more criticism, we may be passive aggressive and ignore what they say, or we may actually do even more of the thing that bothers them just to get back at them or try to prove that we are not in the wrong. Even if we use these tactics unconsciously, defenses of any kind only escalate problems in the relationship.

This does not mean that you lack the right to complain and tell someone when you don't like his or her behavior. However, understanding must precede the complaint or advice and respect for the person. If you want another person to really listen to what you have to say and respect your opinion, you must first show that you respect them through using words of understanding, empathy, and validation. This establishes you as someone safe who does not want to hurt him or her.

A suggestion is just that and not a demand, so harping on a point is just trying to prove you are right, which is conflictual and negative. Have faith in the other person to do what is best for them in that moment. They don't have to take your advice. If they don't take your advice, and they fall on their face, be there for them in a supportive way so they can learn and grow from the experience. "I told you so," is a criticism and is not supportive.

If a person who appreciates you for the person you are makes a suggestion for improvement, you are more likely to listen to that person than someone you think is just criticizing you, pointing out your negatives, or worrying about you unnecessarily because they lack faith in you. When a person is supportive of you, their comments are seen as suggestions and not criticisms.

How do you like people who criticize you? Not much, I'd venture. We don't usually feel good about ourselves when we are around people who are critical of us. We enjoy being around people who accept and appreciate us just the way we are. No one likes a critic! While we can overcome our reaction to them, they may still be at the bottom of our popularity list.

I remember comforting a young teenage girl who was jealous because a new girl was getting all the attention of her friends. When I asked her to describe the new girl, the first characteristic she could think of was how accepting and nonjudgmental the new girl was of everyone. I asked, "Do you like that?" When she replied that she did like it, I asked her if she thought she was that way herself. With a shocked look on her face, she reflected on her own judgmental nature and admitted that, like her friends, she would prefer being around the nonjudgmental girl too. She was a fast learner and began altering her critical attitude, which changed her popularity with her peers.

Origins of Critical Addiction

We are not born critical. Criticism is a learned behavior that does not serve us, yet it is widespread, destructive, and goes unrecognized and undiagnosed as a highly communicable social disease. There are two primary ways we learn criticism: we learn it through our culture, and we learn it through traumatic experiences, which teach us fear and distrust.

There are millions of sufferers who believe that a critical state of mind is a necessary part of being responsible, simply because they were taught to criticize at an early age. This belief has been passed down through generations.

Many people are taught there is something innately wrong with them and that being self-critical will help them improve and become better people. They fear making mistakes, which makes them critical of everything, looking for possible problems as a way to prevent them. Some believe they have to be better than others just to be worthy, so they are constantly comparing and/or competing to prove themselves. Social values support these and other false assumptions, spreading this communicable disease, while criticism erodes the self-esteem of everyone it targets.

Critics are usually people who express the desire to "be good" and "do the right thing." However, no matter how hard they try or what they do, they never feel good enough and never think they have done enough. They must live up to some imaginary standard that seems to constantly change and exist just outside their reach. Sometimes they take solace in the faults and inadequacies of others so that they can feel better about themselves.

Some addicts are self-critical, while others are so afraid of being weak or inadequate that they deny their own mistakes or perceived shortcomings and focus all of their criticism on others. But under this veil of secrecy and denial (and even the appearance of superiority), these critics share the same feelings of inadequacy as the ones who are self-critical.

Habitual criticism paired with negative thinking has gone unrecognized as an addiction in itself, because it is not based on any external dependency and cannot be evaluated on appearances. Critical addiction is an addiction to a thinking process that distorts awareness, destroys self-confidence, and interferes with the ability to enjoy life. Addicts have difficulty enjoying life, because they must be constantly on guard against making mistakes or being the victims of the mistakes of others. Understanding criticism addiction is necessary for the healing of all addictions and social problems. We cannot have peace or real freedom until we see life from a life-affirming perspective.

When we look back with nostalgia on the good old days, we usually remember a time when people appreciated what they had and what they could do. Life was simple. Today, thanks to television and the Internet, we know more about the world and different lifestyles. This is wonderful if you find appreciation for our collective differences, but it is painful if you compare yourself to others. Critics make comparisons, focusing on what they don't have and can't do, instead of noticing what is possible and seeing life from a perspective of abundance.

We are happy when we appreciate what we have and feel grateful for what we can do. This is an attitude of gratitude that is available to everyone while we enjoy the process of creating a better life. We need only to change our perspective—but to change it, we first need to identify the problem and value seeing things differently.

We also learn to be critical as the result of traumatic experiences that leave us with a negative outlook on life. Our society has increasing numbers of people involved in combat, crime, violence, and child abuse who suffer from post-traumatic stress disorder (PTSD) and other forms of trauma. They need professional help to heal. However, trauma distorts perception and causes problems in every area of life, including employment. It is often the people who need help the most that do not have the health care resources to obtain it, resulting in more crime, violence, and drug dependency, perpetuating the problem. Therefore, health care reform is a matter of national security and far less expensive than building more prisons.

Negativity and Illness

I want to add a special note here about illness. It is important to acknowledge that it is more difficult for a sick person to be in a positive state of mind than a healthy person. Because of the direct relationship between body and mind, toxins and disease take a toll on the mind. Some diseases and energy imbalances are especially toxic to the mind, causing people to feel anxious and depressed. Dehydration can also cause depression. So, it is important to drink plenty of water, eat healthy foods, and exercise as part of healing the mind of negativity.

That being said, even though it may very well be more difficult for a sick person to be positive than a healthy one, it is absolutely essential for sick people to take charge of their minds and turn their thinking around if they want to make a full recovery. The shift will help them get well faster and open the door to the possibility of full recovery, instead of just masking symptoms or experiencing temporary relief. We get sick from the outside in, but we get well from the inside out. Our thinking has a huge impact on the body, and focusing on the positive is what plants seeds for miracles. Anyone can do the Four Steps to Freedom found in part three of this book, even if they are ill.

Addictive and Dangerous

Criticism is a guilty pleasure that, once indulged, attracts the user again and again like an addict to a drug. Whenever the critic feels down or has problems, he or she uses criticism like a drug to feel better. It gives the user a false sense of superiority or power over others, even though that power is purely destructive to others and themselves. Not only are they attracted to being critical of others to feel better, but because critical energy is negative, they attract criticism to themselves as well. This perpetuates a vicious, self-destructive cycle as they become the target of criticism from others, lowering their self-esteem and causing them to become even more critical.

Although criticism is not a substance, it is as addictive as any drug, and I propose it poses a threat that is actually more insidious. Habitual criticism has all the characteristics of a drug:

- Criticism is habit forming.
- Criticism is mood altering.
- Criticism can be life threatening.
- Criticism distorts awareness.
- Criticism leads to destructive behavior.
- Criticism adversely affects mental and physical health.

It is truly a social disease that affects whole families, organizations, and societies. Like drug addiction, criticism affects everyone; it affects the person criticizing, the person being criticized, and the people around them. However, there are many aspects of criticism and negativity that present a more insidious danger than drugs, for the reasons that follow.

No Product Involved

Criticism's threat can be considered more insidious than drugs because there is no product involved, making it completely accessible to literally everyone at all times. It is available to the rich and poor alike. Anyone can use it, including young children. In fact, it is an equal opportunity addiction available to every person, regardless of income, age, sex, nationality, education, sexual preference, or political party.

Masked by Social Popularity

Criticism is incredibly dangerous because, like alcohol, the danger of criticism is masked by social popularity. Not only is it socially acceptable to be critical, but people are also expected to participate in criticism at most social functions. Gossiping, faultfinding, worrying, and complaining are national pastimes.

People are offered a sense of belonging when they band together to blame someone or some group for their problems. For example, complaining about the opposite sex can give individuals a sense of comradeship with others of the same sex. As another example, children of divorced parents often feel insecure, criticizing one parent to feel more connected to the parent they are with at the given time.

People habitually complain about their work, family, and government. Sales of newspapers and gossip magazines increase sharply when there is a scandal to report. Virtually anyone who is first to report a scandal or deliver bad news receives special attention.

We also value our critics. Professional critics are paid well for their critiques of politics, movies, books, restaurants, theater, art, etc. There is snob appeal in being a critic who looks down on and degrades what he or she believes to be inferior products, ideals, and people. Sadly enough, our society rewards critics with high salaries, special privileges, respect, and popularity. While there are those in this profession who fairly and respectfully evaluate strengths and weaknesses, they are often the exception instead of the rule.

Unfortunately, those who are more critical appear to get higher ratings and be more popular than their less critical counterparts, possibly because this social disease has become so prevalent. The *Judge Judy* show is a good example. People who feel bad about themselves may get vicarious pleasure out of watching someone like Judge Judy bash people that the viewers perceive to be even more reprehensible than they see themselves to be. There is a reason that this scathingly critical woman is often reported to have the most popular show on television.

Shows in which people are degraded become tantamount to hangouts for critical addicts, because they are attracted to guilt and negativity. Such shows offer them the opportunity to vicariously inflict guilt on others and get a temporary high or sense of superiority out of putting others down. But, at the same time, seeing others hurt triggers their own unhealed memories of being hurt, which feels bad and feeds the addiction, ultimately leaving them filled with even more guilt and negativity. This attracts criticism from others, starting the cycle all over again.

Society Values Criticism

Critical addiction also poses a deceitful threat not carried with drug addiction, because society actually values criticism, judgment, shame, worry, and guilt as productive and necessary. Condemnation of "wrongdoing" is considered to be the right thing to do.

There is an underlying false assumption that if people feel guilty enough, or if they believe that what they are doing is wrong or bad, they will stop doing the unwanted behavior. In other words, most people falsely believe that guilt and shame motivate positive behaviors. Until this insane assumption is challenged and changed, there is no hope for addicts, because the belief justifies frequent faultfinding as the right thing to do.

Do you ever do things you know you will later regret, like eat junk food, drink too much, stay out too late, or tell someone off? Of course you do. We have all done things that we believe are wrong or bad for us. We knew we would feel guilty if we did them, but we did them anyway. Our fear of feeling guilty did not stop us. Knowing that drugs, cigarettes, and alcohol are unhealthy—and may even result in death—does not stop some people from using them.

Neither shame nor guilt motivates people to take positive action. In fact, people who feel shame or guilt are more likely to have destructive behavior than those who feel good about themselves. Shame and guilt only magnify a person's low self-esteem and problems. Drug treatment programs only work long-term when they help people to like themselves.

Mistaken for Problem Solving

Criticism poses a threat because it is mistaken for the productive process of problem solving. A problem exists when there is interference with desired results in a given situation. Therefore, problem solving is a supportive process for considering ways and means to get the results we want or to reach a goal. Problem solving evaluates available resources and skills and how they can be used more productively. It identifies, but does not dwell on, what is lacking in the situation or what can't be done. The problem solving process focuses on solutions; it concentrates on what can be used and what can be done. Unlike critics, problem solvers make suggestions that help people get the results they want without degrading them for the present condition.

While it takes skill to solve problems, anyone can be a critic. Critics seek problems, not solutions. Critics point out limitations and flaws, often without even attempting to pinpoint the recipient's strengths or ways to use those assets to improve performance. Criticism can easily be done by anyone, even those who have no intention of doing anything to improve the situation.

Communicable Social Disease

Criticism is a particularly insidious addiction, as it is a highly contagious and communicable social disease that is also self-replicating. Targets of criticism eventually catch the disease as their self-esteem erodes. People with low self-esteem blame themselves and others, passing on the disease to even more recipients. Thus, the critical addiction of one person spreads to many.

Critical thinking is passed down from one generation to another as the children of addicts are exposed to this critical influence starting at birth. It is sad to see small children already hate themselves and others because they believe the negative things their parents tell them. Adults and mentors may model critical beliefs, attitudes, and ways of thinking. If the people we were brought up to respect are critical, we assume it is desirable to be like them without even realizing how negative they are. Some people have never even known a positive role model.

Used for Social Control

Criticism is dangerous because it produces shame, guilt, and fear, which are used for social control by people and institutions that cannot dominate physically or otherwise. Almost every day, I talk to adults who still suffer from memories of being degraded and humiliated by a schoolteacher. This is sad but true. And it happens far too often.

Historically, might made right, and those with the strongest army conquered and ruled the land. Because of their superior physical strength, some men had all the power, conquering and ruling weaker people by force. Women and weaker men were often helpless to protect themselves from physical abuse, which was allowed in most societies. The vows of church clerics prevented them from being physically dominant and taking up arms against oppressors; their job was to serve others and bring peace, not war. Some women and clerics gained power by being the guardians of moral standards. They were often able to use shame, guilt, and the fear of God to control those over which they had no physical dominance.

Traditionally, mothers and religions have been in charge of our children and their moral education. That tradition continues today. Many people believe they must meet the standards of their religion and parents, and they feel shame when they don't meet these standards. They believe they are not as good as they should be and that they will be punished in some way for their shortcomings. Therefore, it is possible for those who set moral standards to use shame, guilt, and fear for social control.

Evidence of this moral abuse is seen in the common negative stereotype of mothers 'laying guilt trips' on their children. These guilt-tripping mothers are depicted as having a delusional sense of entitlement, which they use when they manipulate and coerce their children with statements like, "How could you do this to me after all I have done for you?"

Condemnation, a particular form of criticism that shames the other, can even be used to control those who are bigger than us or have authority over us. Therefore, small children learn to use condemnation in their defense, and may continue to use it as adults whenever they feel controlled and helpless, resulting in name-calling as a habitual way of protecting themselves.

Children's fairytales are filled with stories of people who are characterized as being either all good or all bad. Many, if not most of these stories, are highly polarized. Good people were always right and did the right thing, while bad people were always wrong and did the wrong thing. This gave us unrealistic standards and expectations of others and ourselves.

Some children conclude that they cannot compete and will never be good enough, because the standards are too high and the path is too difficult and painful. They believe they cannot afford to sacrifice what little they have, so they give up on being 'good' and identify with the 'bad' children in the stories. They are unhappy and grow up with negative self-images, seeing themselves as villains, victims, or both.

I have noticed a welcome trend in some television and movie storylines today. These plots reveal the good qualities that lie within the villain, as well as negative characteristics that plague the hero. Today's

Superman makes mistakes and has a dark side with which he wrestles, while Lex Luthor, the villain, has a heart that was hurt. He frequently tries to do something kind, only to be thwarted in his attempt. This humanizing of people is a progressive change. I don't believe that anyone is all good or all bad. We are just human beings with human frailties that challenge us.

Basis for All Addictions

Criticism is more dangerous than drugs, because critical thinking is the basis for all other addictions, including drugs. Alcohol does not cause alcoholism any more than drugs cause drug addiction. People who feel good typically do not want to consistently alter their awareness. Drugs interfere with their natural high on life.

With the exception of newborns of drug addicted mothers, drugs and alcohol do not cause addiction; they merely keep it going once it has started. These and other addictions are secondary addictions, which are precipitated by a primary addiction. Critical thinking is the underlying primary addiction.

When the pain of criticism (self-inflicted or otherwise), guilt, worry, fear, and shame become too great, most people try to alter their mental state with drugs, sleep, food, shopping, physical activity, or redirected mental and emotional activity. The form of pain relief that they use most becomes an addiction and is their best coping strategy. It is the only way they know to temporarily block negativity from reemerging in their consciousness. The problem is … it doesn't work to stop the mind from being critical. It just causes more issues in their life, perpetuating the cycle.

Symptoms

**Criticism, like germs, spreads dis-ease.
When infected, cover your mouth and
find something to appreciate.**

As a recovery addict of critical addiction, I know that each person suffering from critical addiction has an Inner Critic analyzing and judging their every move, comparing them to others, worrying about the future, making life uncomfortable, and lowering their self-worth. Everyone wants to feel good, but we can't feel good when we are critical of others and ourselves. So we find ways to silence the Inner Critic, even if only temporarily.

How we silence the Inner Critic manifests in a variety of coping strategies and secondary addictions, which are all symptoms of this social disease. These are ten of the most common ways that we silence the Critic. This is not a complete list. I am sure you can think of others.

Perfectionism

People who are addicted to self-criticism often go under the guise of being a perfectionist, which is a virtuous sounding title for an advanced form of this disease. Perfectionists can make it sound like they are part of a superior race of beings that have higher standards than others. They claim they do not expect this excellence from others, while those around them feel pressured to excel, compete, or avoid mistakes.

Some people assume perfectionists think they are better than others, but that is not really true. Perfectionists actually have feelings of lack or insufficiency that they try to hide from themselves and others.

They don't believe they are good enough, do enough, or have enough. They must constantly strive to prove themselves, whether it is with the perfect body, the cleanest house, the highest sales, etc. Perfectionists are driven by criticism addiction and therefore have great difficulty in just letting go, being spontaneous, and having fun. This is because they are suffering from the tyranny of their Inner Critic.

Self-Righteousness, Prejudice, and Bigotry

Self-righteousness, prejudice, and bigotry are all forms of judgment that produce an artificial high by condemning others. This is a highly addictive form of criticism, because it appears to elevate the critics, making them superior to others. It lulls users into a false sense of security in which they erroneously believe that they belong to an elite group that is uniquely qualified to make righteous judgments on others. However, the high they get from judging does not last long, forcing the users to constantly find more people to criticize in order to maintain this good feeling.

Condemnation and looking down on others helps these critics feel better about themselves at the expense of others. It is their fix, because they set the standards for judgment and can exclude anything they do not want to see about themselves. This form of critical addiction has special appeal to some religious people as a way of avoiding self-examination and feeling the effects of their own judgment. I find it very sad that many Christians judge people harshly even though Jesus repeatedly told them not to judge.

Sarcasm

Sarcasm is a covert and seemingly polite way to hide critical and often hostile comments, such as saying, "Don't work too hard" to a person you think is lazy. While those who use sarcasm to hide their hostile feelings may consider this humorous, sarcasm is offensive because it is a veiled attack. Sarcasm also requires a certain level of sophisticated understanding, which may be lacking in people who are very innocent or who have certain forms of brain damage, dementia, and autism. They hear sarcasm as a statement of truth.

When a person is offended by the sarcasm, the critic often blames the victim by making statements like, "I was just kidding," and "You are just too sensitive," or "Can't you take a joke?"

Many highly paid comedians have become famous for their sarcasm in ridiculing people for their looks, ethnicity, shortcomings, and handicaps. The audience participates in this form of cruelty when they laugh at the jokes and the person being humiliated, revealing their own judgmental nature and insecurities.

This type of humor is very different than when a comedian helps us notice characteristics we have in common by laughing *with* us at some of the things we as humans do. George Carlin's famous monologue on "stuff," and how we even buy stuff to put our stuff in, is a great example. It does not attack the character of any person or group, but it instead focuses on common behaviors that are humorous and sometimes even endearing. This kind of humor can be both revealing and healing.

Worrying

Worriers have a critical view of the future with little faith in others. Our society has taught many of us that responsible people worry. Worry is a negative habit that causes some people to feel fearful and anxious, while also feeling important—because they believe they are being responsible for others by worrying about them. They keep their Inner Critic focused on others and finding fault with them. This is quite nonsensical when you think about it. Being fearful does not prevent problems. Worry never paid a bill. Taking action to do something that will change a circumstance is helpful, but simply worrying just produces negative feelings.

Worriers sometimes create a lot of drama, which brings attention to themselves. Seeing impending doom rallies other people to support them. Habitual worriers are often called "worrywarts." They spend their time worrying, often thinking that their worrying is genuinely productive. While worrying does not reap a benefit, it can actually cause a host of physical problems like high blood pressure and stomach issues. On top of that, worriers upset others and typically engage in additional addictions to sooth their fears. Alcohol is a common drug of choice for worriers because it depresses anxiety.

Denial and Secrecy

When people don't own their actions or mistakes, and when they cannot accept responsibility for themselves, they often use denial and secrecy as a self-defense. Denial and secrecy are used in the traditional, macho ideal of manhood. According to this ideal, a man must always be strong, courageous, aggressive, unemotional, and right. Any weakness must be denied. According to this doctrine, a real man is not allowed to have feelings, make mistakes, or be wrong. Emotions, errors, and weakness are hidden with denial and secrecy. Since people do not notice things for which they have no label or frame of reference, many men have not developed an internal dialogue that languages their emotions.

There was a time in history when a man's survival depended on looking outside for the cause of pain so that he could defend against physical attacks. Thankfully, this is rarely true in most civilized societies. More and more, men are allowed to be human, make mistakes, have feelings, and still be considered good, strong men. After all, it takes a strong person to own up to his or her mistakes.

Some women also use denial and secrecy. They are unaware of having self-doubts or feelings of inadequacy and shame, even though they feel the effects of these emotions. They only know that they feel bad, and so they look outside of themselves to find the cause of their pain, blaming others. This habit of projecting blame leads to anger in both men and women.

Unfortunately, denial and secrecy became a traditional way to handle many family problems. When this exists, no one shares their feelings or talks about their feelings or the metaphorical elephant in the living room (like an alcoholic or abusive parent), which is the real problem. Instead, they pretend as though the problem does not exist, despite the fact that it is obvious. This infects everyone involved in the situation as they participate in the deception.

We can deny our problems and shortcomings and do everything possible to hide our mistakes from others. Denial moves perceived faults out of sight, giving us the appearance of peace, even if it is superficial and temporary. However, the problem with this solution is that we really do know what happened and what is going on. We cannot 'not know' what we know, and this knowledge will eat at us deep inside and manifest in undesirable expressions, such as ill health and anger projected onto others.

Anger

Anger is another way to attempt an escape from the Inner Critic. Just project the guilt on others as the cause of our problems. We would be okay if other people would just do what they should do and quit messing us up. Does this sound familiar?

We can wear anger as a punitive mask to make us feel strong when we feel weak, vulnerable, or guilty. Anger hides our vulnerable feelings of hurt, insecurity, shame, helplessness, or inadequacy caused by self-criticism and self-doubt. If you want to know the real source of your anger, ask yourself what you are afraid of or what hurts. Someone else may have hurt you, but the self-doubt that it caused is now the actual source of ongoing anger. It is now self-inflicted by the Inner Critic feeding on your insecurity.

When we can't deal with our vulnerable feelings, we try to blame others for our weakened condition. Attack thoughts fuel our fire as we lash out at whomever we perceive to be the blame, seeking to punish the offender. We may actually be angry with ourselves. If we have denied our own part in a perceived problem, we may project blame on others to protect ourselves from the wrath of our own inner judgment, which keeps us from feeling guilty.

People frequently get a euphoric rush and adrenaline high from their own anger, even though the chemicals produced by the anger are actually destructive to their nervous system and health. Anger has a negative effect on the body for up to six hours after we are no longer angry. Anger is not only abusive to others but to ourselves as well. You can read more about the destructive effect of anger and other negative emotions at www.heartmath.org.

Habitual anger is a particularly dangerous symptom of an advanced stage of critical addiction that has consequences as serious as death itself. I believe that domestic violence and road rage are the result of critical addiction. Anger is used to discipline children and others by making them afraid to make us angry. If habitual anger was publicly recognized as an advanced form of critical addiction, addicts would receive treatment earlier, and the number of injuries and deaths due to domestic violence and road rage would decrease significantly.

Disease

More and more, health practitioners are recognizing the impact that stressors such as anxiety and criticism have on disease. I have met doctors who believe negative thinking is the number one cause of disease. When we stuff or deny our negative emotions, the stressful energy has to go somewhere, so it is held in our bodies. This causes illness and all of the feelings of helplessness and insecurity that go along with poor health. It is well documented that there is an emotional component to all illnesses.

Negativity impacts the body and immune system. It is either expressed emotionally and processed consciously, or it is expressed unconsciously and processed as ill health. Guilt and shame literally eat away at the body's defenses.

Depression

We become depressed when we believe it is not okay to feel what we feel. We depress our anger and vulnerable feelings, believing that it is not okay for us to be angry or hurt. Depression is a mask woven out of apathetic feelings of not caring what happens and a disinterest in life. We tell ourselves that a situation in our life "should be" okay with us and we really "shouldn't be" complaining about it. We may either think there is nothing we can do about the situation or that we would lose something important to our security by complaining or doing something about it.

Not caring feels safer than caring without being able to do anything about it. Depression or loss of emotion can become so strong that we are no longer motivated to struggle for survival. Life itself may seem like too much trouble, which can lead to suicidal thoughts and actions.

Substance Abuse

Critical addiction is a primary addiction that starts as simple self-criticism and frequently escalates into a variety of advanced forms of this social disease. As we mentioned earlier in this book, when the pain of criticism becomes too great, people often seek to alter their awareness through external stimulation or depressing substances, such as drugs and alcohol. Frequently, people go through a recovery program to stop one addiction, only to find that they have replaced one addiction with another addiction ... or they discover they already have other addictions such as co-dependency, love addiction, sex addiction, work addiction, food addiction, etc. The list goes on and on, because the primary addiction—critical addiction—is not being addressed or treated. Critical addition is the underlying cause of all addictions.

Prescription Drugs

We use prescription drugs to control anxiety and depressing thoughts brought on by the Inner Critic. These thoughts can be disabling. Fear and dread are created in our minds by our vivid imagination. We image what might happen in the future, and we imagine that what happened in the past as still happening.

The brain does not know the difference between a physical event and images in our mind, so the body reacts to our mental images as if the events are real. For example, if we expect something dangerous to happen, our body reacts accordingly by producing adrenaline, and we panic even though we may be safely tucked in bed. We use pills to control our emotions, pills to sleep, pills to calm us, pills to give us energy, pills help us focus, etc. The Inner Critic keeps the pharmaceutical industry in business.

Resistance Does Not Work

Attempting to silence the Inner Critic does not work, because if we use any of the preceding coping strategies, we believe the Inner Critic is telling the truth—a truth so foul that we must hide it. By hiding our negative beliefs about ourselves, we actually affirm to our subconscious mind that these judgments must be true. The problem is, when we hide them, we don't question their validity. What if these judgments are wrong? What if we are suffering needlessly? What if we are wrong about these beliefs that hurt us?

When we deflect, disguise, or redirect our attention, we actually cause more problems. For example, when we use criticism or worry to solve our problems, we think it can get us something of value, when in reality we get nothing from it but unhappiness. Recognizing the self-destructiveness of criticism can be a turning point in life.

What We Resist Persists

I was in my early twenties when I first noticed my own critical nature handed down to me through generations of well-meaning puritan souls. My discontent with my husband led me to the uncomfortable recognition of my own critical mind. I noticed that the things I was criticizing my husband for were the same kind of things I disliked in myself. I was projecting my own self-judgment onto him, because it was easier for me to recognize these faults in him than in myself. Every judgment I made of him was actually a judgment on myself.

That revelation filled me with revulsion. I realized that I was just like my parents, and I hated how critical they were. This was not the kind of person I wanted to be. Being critical did not feel good, no matter which person I was judging. Regardless of the target, I was the one who had to live with the negativity.

I decided to take the direct approach and silence my Inner Critic. I would simply stop being critical. I would go cold turkey and kick this nasty habit. I wanted to be free of it once and for all.

I firmly resolved not to be critical any longer, but the harder I tried not to criticize, the more critical I became. Now, not only was I still critical but I was also critical of myself for *being* critical. It became a nightmare as the intensity of my criticisms increased. The end result? I was still critical and judging myself to be a failure as well, because I wasn't accomplishing my goal! It reminded me of the time I tried to stop smoking and all I could think about was how much I wanted a cigarette. I had failed at that too. My negative emotions were spinning out of control.

Without realizing it, I was giving power to criticism by focusing on it as an object of scorn and rejection. There is an old saying … "Whatever you resist persists." I was finding out how true that really is, but I did not know what else to do. I felt like I was drowning in a sea of critical thoughts that bombarded my mind. There was a petty tyrant, and it lived inside of me.

One day, a wise friend said to me, "Kalie, if you don't want to be critical, what do you want to be?" I knew what I did not want, but I had never thought about what I wanted to replace it with.

The idea of being the change I wanted to see was foreign to me. What did I want to be? After thinking about it for only a moment, I happily replied, "I want to be a loving, accepting person."

My friend told me that is it is impossible to admire a quality in someone else that we don't already possess within ourselves, even if we aren't expressing it or have it fully developed. Qualities we value the most are actually qualities that accurately express our true nature. We have a basic need to be ourselves and quite often only recognize our own valuable qualities in others.

Then he said, "As of this day, recognize yourself as a loving, accepting person, because those are the qualities that express who you really are. Now, go live your life as a loving, accepting person, and focus on doing what loving, accepting people do."

Wow! The truth was so simple. That perspective made all the difference in the world. All I had to do was focus on how I wanted to be and claim it as the truth of who and what I am. In each situation, I could ask myself how to handle it with love and acceptance.

As I focused on being more accepting of others and life situations, my life began to change for the better. Do I ever have critical thoughts now? Of course I do, but not often, because my identity changed. Criticism is now out of character for me, as it does not express my real nature and the person I have come to realize I truly am.

Before, I saw myself as a critical person who was trying hard not to criticize—a seemingly impossible task. Now I am aware that I am a loving, accepting person who criticizes only occasionally. That is a big difference.

Anything given energy grows, and anything denied energy dies a natural death. This is a law of physics. We give energy to something when we focus our attention on it. The mental images on which we consistently center tend to manifest in our lives. Even though we may not recognize how it is happening or how we are doing it, the answer is simple. *We create what we think about most of the time.*

The Alchemy of Resistance

The following is one of my favorite stories to explain how resistance affects us. While the story is pure fantasy, the interactive demonstration is real. If you participate with the secret ingredient, you will get more benefits than just reading about it.

Long ago and far away, it was rumored that mighty sorcerers could turn lead into gold through an ancient science called alchemy. This practice was a very controversial and a well-guarded secret, and it remains a secret of powerful people today. If you listen closely, I will reveal this ancient secret to you right now.

First, get a large iron kettle. Into the kettle, pour two quarts of tomato juice and a can of assorted nuts and bolts. Then drop in one small piece of iron, the eye of a gnat, and the wing of a bat. That part is very simple. Almost anyone can do it. However, the next part is the secret ingredient. It will work every single time, producing massive amounts of gold—wealth beyond your wildest imagination—but I warn you that it is nearly impossible to do.

Take a large wooden spoon and stir the contents of this kettle one hundred times without thinking of the word *hippopotamus*. To practice this prior to searching for gnat eyes and bat wings, simply do not think hippopotamus for the next 10 seconds, and see what happens …

Was it easy? No? Of course it wasn't. It was impossible. The harder you try not to think hippopotamus, the more it comes into your mind.

Now, think of the word *giraffe* for the next 10 seconds …

Was that easy? Of course it was! It was very easy. We are always free to think whatever we want to think. Even though our minds may sometimes wander, we can always choose again and bring our attention back to whatever we select. We have a choice.

'Hippopotamus' is the object of the sentence, "Don't think hippopotamus." It is also the object of the sentence, "Think hippopotamus." Since the object of a sentence is also the object of our attention and energy, it does not matter whether we choose to think hippopotamus or if we try to *not* think hippopotamus. Hippopotamus remains the focus of our attention. Remember, a basic law of physics states that whatever we give energy to will grow. So, in this example, our awareness of hippopotamus grows whether we want to think hippopotamus or not.

The same phenomenon happens when we try to stop an old habit or behavior. We focus our attention on what we do not want to experience, which creates the very thing we fear most. Whatever we resist, deny, or suppress persists, because we are giving it energy through the focus of our attention and the power of resistance. Resistance is a powerful and deceptive creator.

But the beautiful thing is that we are always free to choose again. We can choose to redirect our energy and put it into whatever we want, like we did when we decided to think giraffe. Thinking giraffe is easy. Even though the thought of hippopotamus may have popped into our minds from time to time, when there is no strain to resist it, it quickly begins to fade away. We don't resist it, we simply choose to think giraffe instead.

It is important to understand that we aren't making the act of thinking hippopotamus wrong. In fact, we don't place importance on it one way or another. When we don't give it energy, the thought of hippopotamus eventually just fades away, because anything denied energy dies a natural death.

The first step in getting rid of any trait is to choose a replacement for it. This allows us to focus on something specific that we want instead of what we do not want. We can make this choice more powerful by setting our goal in terms of becoming the kind of person we want to be instead of just focusing on changing our behavior, because your identity is the foundation on which all aspects of yourself are built.

In truth, we are already the kind of person we want to be, or we wouldn't value the quality, but because we don't identify with it, we don't express it. Our thinking and behavior change spontaneously when we change our identity. For example, let's take the statement, "I don't want to be critical." A simple replacement would be, "I want to be more accepting," and the identity reframe would be: "I am an accepting person."

Habits are behaviors and can take time, patience, and practice to change, but people can choose to change their identity or the kind of person they want to be at any time. Identification—who and what we think we are—is the foundation of our behavior. If we choose to be caring people, our thinking and behavior will change spontaneously. When we think the way caring people think, we easily do the things that caring people do.

Do you want to be a critical person or an accepting person? What feels better to you? What feels more natural? Which quality do you value?

I had to affirm my own reality to begin the change. The truth is, I am naturally an accepting person, or my criticalness would not have bothered me in the first place. When my thinking was critical, I saw myself as a critical person, which was in conflict with my essential nature. I didn't like myself that way. My thinking was taking me out of integrity with myself. It wasn't natural for me to be critical; it was just the way I was raised to be and the way my parents were raised to be.

The habit of criticism is a way of living that is passed down through generations, so changing this deep pattern of behavior is a major undertaking. I was programmed from birth to be critical by critical parents, as were many of you. I thought it was the right way to be. Since then, I have learned many things that have helped me overcome it.

As I became more caring instead of critical, my world changed for the better. As our society becomes more caring instead of judgmental, our world will change for the better.

As we give more energy to what we want to create instead of what we don't like, we will create more of what we enjoy in our lives. We will get more of what we focus on most of the time. As we give more energy to being kind and treating others with kindness, the world will become a better place.

It is not natural for anyone to be critical. Children are born as loving and accepting beings. Being critical is a learned behavior, and I was willing to unlearn it. Are you?

PART II:

FOCUSING ON THE SOLUTION

Creating Healthy Environments

It is easier to be healthy, productive, and creative in healthy environments. This includes the attitudes of those around us. A friend of mine taught team building classes to government administrators to promote healthier environments for workers. Her presentations were always well received, but she experienced two consistent obstacles. First, there were always a few participants who simply didn't want to be there. Secondly, there were the few who tried to take charge. Both kinds took the same approach. They would criticize each step of the process, thus taking up valuable time with needless explanations in attempting to show that either the class was unnecessary or that they knew more than the teacher did. Ironically, these were the same people who needed the team building skills the most. They were not team players, and their critical attitudes created an unhealthy environment for the other participants.

My friend asked me to observe one of her four-day seminars to see if I could come up with a solution. After watching what happened in her class, I asked her if I could do the opening section for next the class. She agreed to it.

At the beginning of the next class, I presented a chart with two columns on it. The first column was a list of dysfunctional attitudes and behaviors, and the second column was a list of high performance attitudes and behaviors. It worked. No one made a critical remark throughout the rest of the week.

What was my secret? I had simply put *criticism* on the list of dysfunctional behaviors. In other words, I made the act of criticism politically incorrect for this group of administrators. The rest of the seminar was fantastic and enjoyed by all. I had created a healthy environment simply by educating people as to what behavior was healthy and what behavior was not healthy, and no one wanted to look bad in front of others.

What would happen if we could create socially healthy home, school, and work environments? What would it be like if criticism became socially unacceptable and politically incorrect? What if it was no longer acceptable to ridicule or degrade others for our own amusement or any other reason? How would that change our world? How would that change your self-esteem and your life?

The first step to change is identifying the problem. We need to find ways to let people know that critical and negative thinking is not healthy. After all, being critical is just another form of bullying, but people get away with it because it has not been labeled as such. We need to research the effects of critical thinking on health and all social problems, as well as ways to make changes in negative environments. Some of them might even be as simple as posting a sign, like I did with these government administrators.

Recovery Programs

When habitual critical thinking is identified as both an addiction and a social disease, steps can be taken to educate the public and destroy the myth that criticism has value, like we did with cigarettes and co-dependency. There was a time when doctors told patients they needed to smoke to calm their nerves. Now we know that cigarettes cause cancer and are addictive. There was a time when it was considered desirable to have your whole world revolve around pleasing others, and it was romantic to be so attached to another that you couldn't live without them. Now these attitudes are known to be unhealthy, co-dependent, and addictive. We need to see criticism and negativity in the same way so that we treat being critical as unhealthy and create educational programs that develop healthy ways to deal with our life issues. We need recovery programs that can do the following:

1. Identify the symptoms of critical addiction.
2. Recognize the consequences of critical addiction.
3. Create early detection of habitual criticism and negativity in our youth, and intervene through education and counseling.
4. Educate our youth and the public on useful and healthy problem solving strategies.
5. Identify the role critical addiction plays in the creation and maintenance of other problems such as addiction, low self-esteem, disease, and social problems.
6. Develop treatment plans for critical addiction.
7. Include treatment for criticism addiction as a part of all recovery programs to improve their recidivism rate.
8. Create socially healthy home, school, and work environments.

Primary Aspects of Self-Awareness

Recovery programs for critical addiction must focus on developing the three primary aspects of self-awareness: identification, appreciation, and intention—i.e., the basis of perception. A healthy identification is the foundation for both the capacity to appreciate and clarity of intention. All three aspects of self-awareness create our perception and ability to experience the full enjoyment of life.

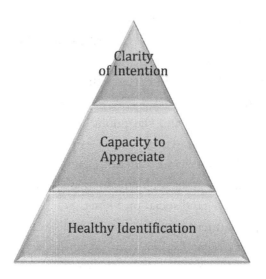

Healthy Identification

Identity is the foundation on which all aspects of the self are built. The capacity to appreciate and create is relative to the kind of person we believe we are. If we are filled with self-doubt and judgments, our awareness will be limited, and we will be unable to appreciate what we have to offer and what we are able to do. This limits our creativity and, therefore, the scope and clarity of our intentions.

The goal of recovery is seeing ourselves differently from the vantage point of a caring, centered place inside of us that is not dependent on what other people think. We need to see ourselves as worthy, valuable, important, and innately good, regardless of our past mistakes and others' opinions. In other words, we need to see ourselves as we were created, with all of our innate qualities intact. This entails the letting go of many layers of false information and painful memories to discover the truth and beauty of our true nature. Then, and only then, can we reclaim our true identity and fully develop the next two qualities.

Capacity to Appreciate

Opening our hearts expands our capacity to appreciate. <u>Our hearts are open the degree to which we allow things to simply be what they are.</u> Judgment blocks our ability to take in information, even when it is right in front of us. If we see anything exactly as it is without judgment, it is just seen as information, and we can appreciate it for what it is and use it appropriately.

The addition of judgment colors our perception and distorts what we see and hear, rendering us incapable of actually listening to what others have to say or seeing what they have to offer, because we have prejudged them. This leaves us with faulty information while others feel unheard and unseen, spreading the disease.

Clarity of Intention

Clarity is necessary for goal setting. That said, clarity only comes from being fully aware of the way things are in the present, as well as understanding the possibility of how things can be in the future. You can't see clearly if your picture is distorted by faulty assumptions about what you are or the inability to appreciate what you and others are capable of doing. Clarity is based on a healthy identity and the capacity to appreciate.

We are all born with the power to create. But without clear intention, this power is like allowing an untrained puppy free to run amok. It chews up things we love and innocently creates a destructive impact on everything around it, instead of simply generating love and appreciation. We need to focus this power in order to create the outcomes that we really want.

When free from the self-destruction of critical addiction, self-esteem blossoms, and the obstacles we once saw as insurmountable simply disappear. While addicted, we continue to exist in the abyss of low self-esteem, where goals are limited, because we don't think we can amount to much or accomplish anything of any real merit. We don't expect much out of life, and we get just what we expect.

Aspects of Identification

So, what is this Inner Critic? Where does it come from? Were we born with it? Isn't it just part of human nature? Can we get rid of it? Do we want to get rid of it? Is it part of us? How did we get this way? Aren't judgments necessary to do our jobs and protect us? These are all good questions, and questions that you may be asking by now.

Did we have a unique identity when we came into this world? Perhaps, but we have to discover it, because when we were born, we were immersed in the emotional and social energy fields of our parents or caretakers. We felt their feelings, emotions, and attitudes as our own.

We had basic needs to be loved, nurtured, and fed; to be kept safe from harm; and to know ourselves. It was up to our caretakers to do most of this for a very long time, but discovering our identity was up to us from the beginning. Self-discovery is something we began to do the moment we were born.

False Identity/Ego

One of the ways in which we get to know ourselves is through feedback, whether the feedback is accurate or not. For example, if you want to know what you look like, you look in a mirror, which gives you feedback. However, the mirror can distort the image and is only two dimensional, so it cannot accurately reflect you as a three dimensional being. We also get feedback from others when they communicate how they see us, which can also be distorted. They may do this through words or facial expressions.

People look at a baby and smile or frown, say loving or derogatory things, and either caress or harm them with touch. From the behavior of its caretakers, the baby concludes that he or she is cute and adorable or bad and a brat, etc. Each piece of feedback is added to the self-image. So, much like pieces of paper mache or lumps of clay, this feedback molds and shapes the baby's self-image.

This self-portrait is not accurate, however, because it is made out of other people's opinions and judgments, which in turn are colored by their own wounds, misperceptions, projections, biases, and ignorance. Nevertheless, this false self-image is what we wear as our identity, which is called an ego. The ego is a false image of what and who we think we are. Awakening or becoming enlightened is an exciting process of loving, forgiving, releasing, transforming, and embracing to discover our real identity and Authentic Self. In part four of this book, we will explore the concept of your Authentic Self and how to tell the difference between your ego (or false self) and your Authentic Self ... the real you.

Social Function of Mirror Neurons

Our brains house multiple mirror neuron systems that have a social function. Mirror neurons copy what they see. They carry out and understand not only the actions of other people, but also others' intentions, as well as the social meaning of others' behaviors and emotions. Mirror neurons make templates for strings of actions linked to intentions. These templates predict what comes next based upon past actions observed, thus passing on social and cultural attitudes, beliefs, and behaviors. Empathy and social emotions like guilt, shame, pride, embarrassment, disgust, and lust are all based upon these mirror neuron systems.

Mirror neuron systems help us learn by watching others. Whenever we watch an action, our brains automatically simulate that action, making templates of each series of actions. The result is recorded as the intention, or purpose for the action, giving it a meaning. Our brains copy what we see happening to help us understand the goal of the action and the emotions involved, which gives us empathy for others. Mirror neurons read minds and emotions through our inner library of recorded templates. They are also responsible for passing on cultural norms.

> In a study published in March 2005 in Public Library of Science, Dr. Iacoboni and his colleagues reported that mirror neurons could discern if another person who was picking up a cup of tea planned to drink from it or clear it from the table. "Mirror neurons provide a powerful biological foundation for the evolution of culture," said Patricia Greenfield, a psychologist at the U.C.L.A. who studies human development.[2]

The same mirror neurons fire off whether we are the one performing an action or we are watching someone else do so. People who have a very active mirror neuron system are very empathetic and sensitive to the plight of others. Empathy allows us to learn vicariously through the actions and emotions of others, without having to directly experience the events ourselves. Empathy can be a very handy way to learn.

Mirror neurons are significant and relevant to understanding critical addiction as a social disease, because they reveal the source of our inner messages as coming from the mirror neuron system hardwired into our brains. Mirror neurons express themselves as what I call either a person's Inner Critic or Inner Coach, depending on the kind of messages they deliver. Furthermore, these messages are reflections of our society, which can manifest as social disease if the messages are destructive in nature.

Mirror neurons absorb culture directly and pass it on to future generations. They become messengers for our caregivers and other significant influences, because mirror neurons continue to repeat what we saw these people doing and heard them saying throughout our lifetime. When mirror neurons hear messages like, "Don't think too well of yourself," "You're not good enough," "You're bad," or "You're spoiled rotten," they repeat those critical messages through an internal dialogue, which I call the Inner Critic. I use the word *hear*, but regardless

---

2   Sandra Blakeslee, "Mirror Neurons: Cells that Read Minds", New York Times, January 10, 2006

of the words they use, the mirror neurons actually reflect what our caregivers modeled. We teach what we live.

Some children hear supportive messages from their caregivers, and their internal dialogue sounds more like an Inner Coach mirroring empowering messages like, "You can do anything you set your mind to do." The Inner Coach continually motivates the person to do great things with their life, resulting in high self-esteem, creativity, good health, and productivity, because the Inner Coach attributes positive meanings to experiences. Knowing this, we can choose to implant loving and supportive messages in our children and ourselves. We can consciously work to develop our own Inner Coach and undo some of the old destructive messages left by destructive programming. It is never too late for us to create new messages.

A child has no way to filter the messages of the Inner Critic and therefore hears them as absolute truth. Children are loyal and want to please their caretakers, so they will behave accordingly, even if that means behaving badly and getting punished for it, just as their parents predicted they would.

When a child is abused, their mirror neurons constantly deliver the abuser's messages, even when the abuser is removed from his or her life. Removing and punishing the abuser does not stop the messages from being delivered daily, because the abuser lives inside the child's mind and body. The mirror neurons will repeat the abusive messages throughout his or her life unless these programs are disrupted and replaced with new, positive programs by transformational processes like EFT (Emotional Freedom Technique), Faster EFT, and EMDR (Eye Movement Desensitization and Reprocessing). These are just a few of the techniques I use in counseling. The reasoning behind this is simple and clear—these messages are not just in their heads; these messages are encoded energetically in their bodies. (You can find more information about these techniques on my website at www.OpenHeartResources. com.)

As adults, we can begin to filter these messages and throw out the lies while we heal the body. The problem is, we have heard the lies for so long that we don't know the lies from the truth. We may feel disloyal, even now, if we go against our programming or what our parents and/ or religion told us to believe, so this is not easy.

Supporting an Inner Coach

The good news is that new mirrors neurons are being created every day, so we can use them to create or support an Inner Coach that will help us replace those dysfunctional messages. This Inner Coach can become even more powerful than the Inner Critic, helping us to discover our own, real Authentic Self.

Since the brain does not know the difference between images in your mind and physical events, you can practice this skill in a very easy way. Watch videos of people doing what you want to do, while imagining that you are performing the same actions yourself. There are many training videos in sports that effectively use this technique. An athlete watches the video many times and imagines that he or she is the one completing the action without incident each time, so that when he or she actually performs the physical action, it is done perfectly. Mirror neurons make this possible.

Saying affirmations is another way to bring positive beliefs into your unconscious mind through repetition. It is important, however, that you affirm what you know in your heart to be true, even if you have never experienced it.

People often try to make something true because they say it many times, like, "I am a millionaire." I have not found this to be successful. For example, in my "What We Resist Persists" chapter, I realized that when I was critical, it didn't feel good to me. It didn't feel natural. However, when I was loving and accepting, it felt great. After that, I affirmed what I preferred to be true of the two experiences, "I am a loving and accepting person," even when I was being critical, and that reminded me of the truth about myself. It gave me a chance to choose again. I am in charge of my destiny; my mirror neurons are not in charge.

Affirming what you are is the most powerful affirmation you can make, because your identity is the foundation on which all aspects of yourself are built. The secret of yogic powers is in affirming a quality of being, like affirming, "I am abundant." As a result of being abundant, you have more than you need of everything you need. You have enough to give away. In fact, giving to others is an affirmation of your abundance. Affirming a quality of being, as in the abundance example above, magnifies it within yourself and helps you to extend it into everything you do.

To begin affirming that you are abundant, you would have to recognize having some experiences of abundance. You would have to be grateful for what you have, because affirmations need to be positive statements of what you have experienced as true. Even though you may doubt that experience of truth when you are upset or feeling down, when you are feeling good, you know it is true.

Once in a while, I run across someone who says they have no positive experiences of feeling good about themselves. I find that often happens to very strong people who have had their strengths discounted by their caretakers as a way of controlling or demeaning them. For example, whether you think a person is stubborn or persistent will depend on whether you like what they are doing or not, but it is the same quality.

If you haven't had any positive experiences of feeling good about yourself, you may need to find a loving, supportive coach or therapist who can help you discover your value. I believe it is a therapist's job to help you discover your strengths and help you affirm them. Unfortunately, some therapists assume they are supposed to point out what is wrong with you and fix you. That assumption is the problem that brought you to need a therapist in the first place, not the solution. You assume something is wrong with you—that you are broken. There are no broken people. You just need someone to help you discover what is right with you and empower you to focus on and use your strengths.

As we grow and develop, we learn new information that can and should replace old beliefs, like the negative feedback we may have received as children. However, the simple act of believing new information is not enough to replace the old beliefs, because you have years of memories and emotions associated with those beliefs. When you are feeling blue, the old beliefs come up to haunt you … and when you are vulnerable, you may believe them. So it is important to discount the old beliefs and implant new beliefs, reinforcing them with positive affirmations that you can call on in times of need. These affirmations will remind you of what you know to be true and good, instead of destructive and negative.

Psych-K is one of the best techniques I know to plant affirmations at a deep, unconscious level, bypassing the logical mind. In Psych-K, you assume a whole-brain posture while making your affirmations, so your mind accepts the affirmation unconditionally. I find it very effective. You can find out more about it by referencing the Holistic Counseling tab on my website at www.OpenHeartResources.com.

Changing Programs

Years ago, I counseled a 78-year-old female client who was grumpy, abrasive, and critical. At the beginning of our first session, she loudly announced that she wanted to die. She said it defiantly, as if she wanted a specific reaction out of me. I told her that was fine with me, but that I was interested in knowing what she wanted to do before she died. My acceptance of her goal surprised and pleased her. We created a plan and began working together to accomplish her goals.

Two weeks later, I got a frantic call from her. She was in the hospital again. Her mental and physical condition had gotten worse. The doctor had decided she was hopelessly senile, and her family was going to put her in a care home. They had given her one month to prepare for the move. She loudly demanded, "You have to do something!"

Having no idea what to do, I asked my inner guidance for help as I was driving to her home to make a house call. It came to me that she had a battle going on between her mind and body. She was a grouchy old woman who was very angry with her body for letting her down. She was an author of five books, a world traveler, and she was not ready to quit. Her previous physical episodes made her furious.

I have come to believe that senility manifests when a person is so critical of his or her physical body and its ability to perform, that the attacks on the body break down the connection between mind and body. Growing older can be very difficult, especially if you value yourself for your physical looks and/or physical and mental agility. When body parts don't work the way they used to, the decline can be experienced as a difficult loss.

Based on this assumption, I created a plan of action. I needed to help her make peace with her body, thus allowing mind and body to work harmoniously together as a team. When I shared my assumption with her, she said she was willing to do anything that might bring about a healing, even if that meant being kind to her body. That was quite a concession from her.

She was weak and partially bedfast when I arrived, so I had to work within those limitations. Luckily, she had already learned a series of exercises to do in bed, so I simply added conscious-connected breathing to her exercises. This meant that she had to breathe a particular way in coordination with her body movements, integrating her body and mind in the following manner ...

She was to inhale with effort as she tensed her muscles on the inward portion of the exercise's movement—and exhale effortlessly as she completed the outward movement or relaxing motion of each exercise. This exhale teaches us how to surrender. The challenge for her was in the exhale, because she had to *allow* the breath to leave her body without pushing it out and without metering it out in a controlled way, which was her habit in everything. This was so difficult for her that it took us an hour just for her to learn how to do two movements in a row. Her goal was to accomplish an entire set of exercises while performing consciousness-connected breathing. She was very determined, and by the following week, she could perform the entire set without pausing.

I also had her start a gratitude journal. Every day she was to write down at least three things that made her feel grateful. Bitterly complaining about this exercise, she begrudgingly found things that she felt warranted an expression of gratitude. Each day her list got longer, and I began seeing traces of a smile that crossed her face from time to time.

When she was able to get out of bed, I asked her to go for walks while chanting, "I can do it" in rhythm with her breath, putting the accent on different words as she went. "**I** can do it. I **can** do it. I can **do** it. I can do **it**." This required even more integration of body and mind.

Be assured that this is a great exercise for anyone, because one of the most destructive critical programs is in believing "I can't." That thought can be so all-pervasive that it affects literally every action a person takes. I have found this unfortunate, negative program in most people who come to see me. It is a short version of all other negative programs that make people feel like victims. The "I can do it" chant is an amazingly simple and fun way to make changes.

Six months later, this woman had finished writing her sixth book and was traveling to Paris to do research for her seventh book. This amazing woman, who became loving and respectful to all parts of herself, lived ten more years. We are never too old to change our programming. Old dogs do learn new tricks.

Discernment Versus Judgment

Because each of us has a false identity to some degree, the ego compares everything we see to our past experiences, judging things as good or bad, more or less, worse or better, etc. Comparisons can only generate judgments of "less than" or "more than"—not real understanding. To judge, we must place more value on some things than others, so we never see anything just as it is. We see life through a distorted view of reality. The ego is insecure, comparing itself to others so that it can find meaning to justify the importance of its own existence. Based on this distortion, it also gives very bad advice.

Judgments involve comparisons between things that may or may not even exist. For example, if I judge someone as being weak, I can only do that by comparing that person to my idea of a strong person. This idea may be unrealistic and imaginary. For example, most men may seem lacking if we compare them to a professional athlete, screen idol, or the Prince Charming portrayed in our fairytales.

Since we have to evaluate our world in some way, it is important that we know the difference between judging and discerning. Judgments limit perception, while discernment expands awareness and accelerates creativity. For example, I can discern the difference between a brunette and a blond, without making a judgment. The moment I assume that blonds are smarter or better than brunettes, I have made a judgment that taints and distorts my ability to see and evaluate blonds or brunettes on their own merit. I am now wearing blinders that distort my view of both.

There is a common distorted view of love and what it means to "be in your heart." Some think that being in your heart or loving means acting mushy, cheery, and soft, or wearing blinders to reality. In reality, it is just the opposite. No one can define love, because defining it would be to limit it, and it is unlimited. However, I do know that love is honest, open, and direct. It does not support illusions of any kind. One thing is totally true about love … love is fear-less. There is no fear in love.

For those of you who are familiar with the chakra system, the heart chakra is at the center of our energy body and integrates all emotions. With care and compassion, it allows all emotions to be okay. The heart is open the degree to which we allow things to simply be what they are.

We are not our false identities, our egos, our wounds, or our programming. And as our hearts begin to open, we discover our true nature. When we are centered in our hearts, we are being authentic. From there, we can discern the truth because we are simply witnessing what is present, free of all judgments and comparisons. Learning to discern what is present helps us reach this state more quickly. This is where real freedom is found.

I had a client bring her boyfriend to one of her sessions with me, and all he could do was complain about his "asshole" brother. After a while, he looked up at me and said, "You aren't going to give me any of the goody two shoes, love and forgiveness crap, are you?"

I said, "No, but would you be willing to just accept your brother as an asshole?" He laughed and said he could do that. Once he accepted his brother as simply being the way he was, the problems between them disappeared. The problem only existed as long as he thought his brother should be something that he wasn't.

Truth Versus Assumption

Most of the time, we make judgments—assumptions about others and life—without really knowing the truth. We live in the world of our own assumptions and conclusions. Some are true. Some are false.

We assume our future, even though we don't really know what it is. We project our past experiences forward in time, expecting similar experiences, and then wonder why history repeats itself. We assume people's motives for doing what they do, while we usually don't even know why we do what *we* do, much less why others do what they do. We assume we know how others feel, which we cannot do with absolute certainty—and we make these assumptions regarding how others feel while we may not even know how we actually feel, ourselves. Whether our judgments and conclusions are true or false, they are all just assumptions and not facts.

I am sure you have had what I call a light bulb experience—one of those moments in which a cartoonist would have undoubtedly drawn a light bulb over your head to signal a bright idea. Everyone has had them. How did it feel?

In having asked that question of many people, I invariably get the same answer. People use different words, but regardless of how they express it, they always say it felt good. This bright idea usually comes with a sigh of relief or an exclamation of "Ah, I get it." This universal experience demonstrates that truth always feels good in the moment we recognize it.

Later, we may make some assumptions about it that don't feel so good. But in the moment of discovery, before we distort this awareness with more assumptions, truth always feels good. Everyone has a built in truth meter, and we instinctually know truth when we hear it.

Truth and peace are inseparable. They are always found together, because knowing the truth brings us peace, and when we are at peace, we know the truth. We are relieved to know the truth, even when it is not something we want to hear. Knowing the truth sets us free to move on with our lives.

If knowing the truth always brings peace, then any painful assumption cannot be true. Therefore, negative assumptions of any kind cannot be true. This is good to know. While the assumption may contain some factual information, the message distorts the truth. It is like looking at the world through dark glasses that color everything we see with darkness.

While it may be a fact that someone you love died, your sadness is about the assumptions you make as a result of their death. You may assume you will always be alone, that the pain you feel will always be there, or that death is the end of all existence, etc. Those fears are assumptions that may change with time or personal growth, while the fact that the person died will not change. It only causes more pain if you try to prove you are right about any of theses assumptions.

Believing that negative assumptions are distortions of reality is a huge departure from how we normally think. However, if you begin challenging yourself to make this simple distinction, you may be surprised at what you discover. People who come to understand how this concept works have experienced major transformations in their lives.

PART III:
HOW TO FIND PEACE

The Desire for Happiness

Everyone wants to be happy. It is natural to want the freedom to be yourself without defending who or what you are. This is not a selfish desire. When you are happy, it helps the people around you. People who love us tend to feel responsible for our state of mind, even though they aren't. If we are happy, they feel better. So, even though you can't make other people happy, when you are happy, most everyone around you benefits. (If a significant person in your life doesn't want you to be happy, then you may need to rethink the relationship. It may not be healthy for you to be around this person.) When you are happy, you feel free to do your best in every area of life. Happiness is a practical idea and a very simple goal for life that brings real freedom.

Our forefathers must have thought happiness was an important part of freedom, because the Declaration of Independence states that our Creator endowed us with certain unalienable Rights, which includes the right to pursue happiness. However, the pursuit and eventual finding of happiness is up to us.

If our goal is happiness, and if criticism, fear, and guilt lower our self-esteem, then these things are not helpful to us in reaching our goal. They have no real value. In fact, negativity of any kind is not useful in the pursuit of happiness. Negativity even gets in the way of simple survival. Since we are free to think whatever we want, it would be useful to discount and devalue all negative or fearful assumptions and messages, and get rid of them. They are not true, because truth always feels good. So they serve no useful purpose. Getting rid of them, however, may not be so simple.

Most everyone has experienced trauma of some kind in his or her life, and I am not suggesting that you should deny what you feel or have experienced. I am suggesting that these kinds of experiences can leave you with negative assumptions about yourself that need healing. However, unless you recognize the nature of these negative assumptions as false, you will assume they are true and you will not seek healing. I will suggest ways you can go about this, but you may also need professional help.

I am also suggesting that you find other ways to process current events in your life. There is a difference between noticing negative events or conditions in the world and making critical assumptions about these events that leave you feeling helpless, guilty, or fearful. You may or may not be able to change the situation, but you can always change the way you see it, which might also lead to you taking action to change it. When tragedy strikes, the people who focus on what they can do to help themselves and others actually heal faster than those who just feel sorry for themselves.

Regardless of the circumstances in your life, you are free to choose how you want to think about the events, and how you think about them can make the difference between being at peace or in a state of conflict. This is the discovery that many great people have made in the midst of extreme conditions, like being prisoners of war. They discovered that they were still free to be at peace in their own minds.

In fact, I taught transcendental meditation in a maximum-security prison to their worst offenders as an experiment to see if meditation made any significant changes in the prisoners. The changes were definitely significant. However, what I remember most about the experiment was one prisoner's experience. He wrote that he came to realize the real bars were on his mind, and now he was free—even though he was still in prison—because he was at peace.

Four Steps to Freedom

The Four Steps to Freedom are simple. They could be summarized as: <u>Let go of what you do not want, and choose what you do want.</u>

While simple does not always mean easy, as is the case here, this does get considerably easier the more you do it. I like to equate it with what happens when a space shuttle blasts off for the moon.

Have you ever watched the launch of the space shuttle? Did you notice how slow it was at first? It couldn't have been going more than five miles per hour when it launched. It went so slow that it looked like it would never make it off the ground, much less all the way to the moon, because it had to break free from the inertia of gravity and the earth.

Just like that space shuttle, we have to break free from the inertia of our old habits, and that takes a lot of effort. We have to break free again and again. We have to choose peace, and then we have to choose peace again and again and again, until finally there is no more choosing and we break free from the bondage of old habits.

Once the space shuttle breaks free from the earth, it drops its fuel tanks, because there is no need to carry that big load anymore. We too need not carry our load of grievances and critical messages. They fuel our angry fire and weigh us down with the gravity of each situation.

In the next stage, the space shuttle flies freely toward the moon. Nevertheless, it still has to fire its rockets and make course corrections every few seconds to stay on target, and so do we. We need to be vigilant for peace in order for us to remain free, because circumstances are always changing. Choosing for peace doesn't end until we reach our destination, and then there is no more choosing.

What I am presenting is a framework of steps needed to break free from the tyranny of the Inner Critic's bondage. There are many paths to peace, but the way the mind works for each path is the same. Use any method or technique that helps you take each step.

A word of caution, however. Make sure the path you choose is actually freeing you. Don't trade in your childhood belief system for another belief system that is also judgmental, which limits you. I have seen many people rebel from their past by using condemnation and resistance, which is a state of mind that is just as dysfunctional as (if not worse than) the state they were in before. Without realizing it, they fuel the angry fire of their Inner Critic to help them rebel against others, instead of replacing the Inner Critic with an Inner Coach and freeing themselves of their inner bondage. This happens when people are not aware that the real problem is within their own mind.

Here is a list of the Four Steps to Freedom. Each of the following chapters will explain exactly how each step works as we explore the world behind the eyes and take a look at how the mind works. The steps are simple, but the Inner Critic tries to complicate them, so educate yourself by reading the chapters carefully. Your mind is a fascinating place to explore, but it can also be deceptive.

1. **Own It**: Notice your feelings, recognizing that the problem is in your mind, which gives you the ability to change it.
2. **Devalue It:** Recognize that any form of negativity has no value.
3. **Flip It**: Release negatives and choose peace.
4. **Replace It:** Focus on something of real value to you.

Use these Four Steps to Freedom, and you will rapidly replace the old way of thinking with ideas that help you feel good about yourself and others. You will also see new opportunities for happiness. This process creates new habits of optimistic thinking, as well as awareness for aspects of life that you may have never seen before. New habits don't materialize overnight, but the benefits certainly accrue as you grow stronger with each and every day.

Step One: Own It

Recognizing that the problem is in your mind gives you the ability to change it. If it is not your problem, you can't solve it—so taking ownership is essential. The purpose of this chapter is to break down this concept even further, so that you're able to see exactly how you can take charge of your own state of mind.

Notice When You Don't Like the Way You Feel

This may sound too simple, but most people are not very self-aware. Awareness of where you are in the present is absolutely necessary before you can choose where you want to go in the future. You need to know your present location before you can map a trip to New York, California, or any other destination.

Few people hold a sufficient level of self-awareness to actually notice how they feel in the present moment. People are either reliving a past experience in their mind, projecting into the future, or focused outside themselves on what they do or don't like. They move through their day without ever noticing their present state of mind or how they feel, even though they may be complaining about their life. Self-awareness is essential for any real change.

Notice when you feel good and when you feel bad … and what you are thinking about in both states. For example, I have found that when I don't like the way I feel, I am often trying to get something or trying to figure out why I am not getting it, and I am making lots of assumptions in the process. When I like the way I feel, I am usually focused on what I have to give or just giving it.

Recognize the Problem Is in Your Mind

Events happen in the world, but your emotions and how you feel about events are personal and are created in your mind. How you feel about events depends on the way you see life and what you believe to be true. Notice that negative emotions like self-doubt, anger, guilt, worry, anxiety, shame, pride, embarrassment, and disgust are coming from judgments made from within your own mind. There is an internal, critical part of your mind that watches and judges you and others.

If the Critic is in your mind, then you are free to change it. If the source of your pain were outside of you, you would truly be a victim because you would be helpless to change it. If someone else has to change for you to feel good, then you will still be a victim, even if they change. You may be a happy victim, but still a victim, because you are dependent on someone else for your happiness.

Even if others are criticizing you, there is nothing they can say that is as damaging as your own criticisms of yourself. When the words of others bother you, they are saying something that part of you believes is true. For example, if I accused you of being a serial killer, you would probably just laugh at me. You wouldn't get defensive or feel bad, because the accusation is so baseless. It is just plain silly. I doubt if you have ever thought of yourself as a serial killer. However, if I were to call you stupid, fat, ugly, weak, or some other such name that you have used to criticize yourself in the past, you would likely feel hurt or defensive. It is your own judgments that hurt you more than anyone else can. When we heal and learn to love and accept ourselves, we raise our self-esteem. Then the opinions of others have less of an effect on us.

Notice that self-judgments are like tape loops that repeat messages from the past. Perhaps you can even remember when you first heard or made a particular judgment, or maybe you remember the person who judged you that way. Perhaps you have no memory of how it started, but the judgment is familiar and has played over and over again throughout your life. Each judgment is a dysfunctional short circuit in your mind.

You may see yourself as critical and even hurt by these judgments or messages without really noticing where they come from. The source is internal. It is the messenger from the past that I call the Inner Critic, which has an identity all its own. Let's shine a spotlight on it, recognizing it for what it really is. <u>The Inner Critic has been talking to you your whole life, but you have probably never recognized that it has an identity completely separate from what you are</u>.

Next, we simply watch its behavior without judging it ... so that we expand our awareness to include it as simply being there. It exists. No judgments. You are not wrong for having one, but you are now aware of having one, which has a great advantage.

Please understand that we have several objectives here, but the most important one is to recognize that the Inner Critic is not you. The Inner Critic is your programming and your wounds, but it is not what you are. This distinct difference is very important. You are not responsible for its being there, so you don't need to be embarrassed by its judgmental nature. However, even though you didn't make it the way it is, you are the only one who can change it.

Years ago, I heard a lecture by Meredith Young-Sowers of The Stillpoint Foundation in which she said, "We get sick from the outside in, but we get well from the inside out." That statement struck me as being profoundly true. It clarifies our responsibility for our own health and wellbeing. We get sick from the outside in, so we are often innocent of causing our own illnesses or state of mind, but we do have a choice regarding what we do about it, and we are responsible for getting well. We can choose to take the steps necessary to get well, and that process happens from the inside out.

No one would consciously choose to be sick physically, mentally, or emotionally, but we live in a world that is polluted physically, emotionally, and energetically by the negativity of our family, society, and the environment. These pollutants have an impact on our minds and bodies that comes to us unbidden.

Unhealthy thoughts also come to us unbidden. They pop into our minds spontaneously. Some emerge when external events trigger old wounds. Some come from toxins in our bodies. Others are mirror neurons firing off old messages, perhaps even from childhood. We also pick up unhealthy ideas from our society, ideas which spread the social disease called critical addiction.

These unhealthy thoughts affect our health and wellbeing. It is not appropriate for us to feel guilty about having these thoughts. We don't have a choice over the thoughts that come into our minds. However, we do have a choice about what we do with them. We can dwell on them, let them go, or transform them. In these Four Steps to Freedom, you will learn ways to heal old wounds and replace negative thoughts with ideas that bring you peace.

Name Your Inner Critic

Since your Inner Critic is not really you, give it an identity that is separate from you by naming it. Separating your awareness of what you are from that of the Inner Critic will change your perspective on the messages it gives, as well as whether you want to believe the messages or not. This experience can be life changing. Become aware of yourself as the *observer* of the Critic—the one who is watching it, not the one who IS the Critic.

Who can observe the Inner Critic without judging it? Only your real, Authentic Self can simply observe it or just notice it. You are the observer, and this is the beginning of your training to witness the world behind the eyes, also known as your internal world. The ability to witness without judging is one of the first characteristics of enlightenment, and it can be consciously developed. Witnessing is an awareness you can develop to speed up the awakening process. It may take practice, but you can learn to do it. Be patient.

The Inner Critic is not your enemy. It is just mindless programming that needs to be recognized for what it is before you can be happy and free. It is the body's reactive way of trying to protect itself by reliving and repeating the past. The Critic is like a robot on automatic, giving false warnings and bad advice. Your programing is also made up of your unresolved wounds and unhealed places, so be companionate with your painful emotions and wounded inner child, but don't let the Critic control your life. Remember, if you judge it, you become like it, and that is not what you want to be.

Understand that the Inner Critic is not wise enough to be in charge of your life. While the ego or Inner Critic is purely reactive, you have the freewill and ability to choose what you want to create in your life. The Inner Critic cannot choose. It just reacts according to past programs, so if it is left in charge, you will repeat your past. You have to take charge if you want a future different than your past. You have to take charge if you want to be free.

Be sure to give yourself awareness points for noticing when your Inner Critic is talking to you. When people first start noticing their Inner Critic, they frequently view themselves negatively for having it and housing its critical messages. But don't let criticism beget more criticism here. Instead, remember that we all have one. This dialogue has gone on your whole life, and you are now becoming aware of it, so don't judge yourself or the Critic for existing. This is just a natural, normal part of life. Give yourself credit for waking up to its existence and being able to see it for what it is without judgment. This is a great accomplishment!

Caution: The ego and Inner Critic will divide and multiply to maintain its existence. You will know that it has multiplied if you find yourself judging, criticizing, or fighting with the Inner Critic. You don't need to defend yourself, but the Critic needs to defend itself, because it has no reality beyond the limited beliefs you have about yourself. Remember, the ego is just a false self-image. It is not real.

You may suddenly find yourself with a Critic and a Judge, both just different aspects of your ego as they carry on an internal dialogue, which sounds like you fighting with yourself. When you see this is happening, just notice it and then simply let it go. This may happen many times during your developmental process here, so just let it be what it is—a learning experience. Again, be grateful that you noticed it and give yourself credit for your awareness.

Observing the Inner Critic will change it, because observation changes that which is being observed. This observer effect has been well documented, and the mistaken idea that anyone can be an objective observer has been thoroughly discredited. A thief cannot steal without incident while people are watching him or her. Even at the subatomic level, particles change when they are observed. The Inner Critic cannot be spontaneous when you are observing it, so simply observing it will disrupt its critical function.

When you weren't watching your Inner Critic, it was doing what critics do, spontaneously and without disruption. It was hurting you, but it was doing so from behind the scenes. It will be much more difficult for the Critic to be destructive while you watch it.

Step Two: Devalue It

**Criticism addicts are attracted to negativity
like moths are attracted to a flame,
because they value it.**

Negativity

Just as alcoholism is a compelling attraction to alcohol, and heroin addiction is a compelling attraction to heroine, <u>critical addiction is a compelling attraction to negativity</u>. Negativity is the food of the Inner Critic that perpetuates this social disease. Negativity is the attractive substance of this addiction.

The attraction to negativity is what makes critical addiction such an insidious disease. Addicts seek negativity and attract it to themselves—without realizing that is what they are doing—because they were taught that negativity has value. As I pointed out in the first chapter, our society values negativity in the forms of criticism, guilt, and fear. As long as we value them, we will attract negativity into our lives. This step is about discounting the value of internal and external negative messages. So, as you might guess, your ego and Inner Critic will not like this step and may argue with it intensely.

The Wizard of Oz offers a great metaphor that illustrates how blind we can be to our strengths while also valuing negative things that scare us. Like the characters in Oz, we can be unaware of our real strengths. The Tin Man longed for a heart, the Scarecrow longed for brains, and the Cowardly Lion longed for courage. They did so, not because they lacked the qualities, but because they valued them and didn't know those qualities were already within themselves. Dorothy also discovered that what she wanted most, to go home, was already within her ability. It is important to note that they didn't discover these authentic qualities until after they had faced their fears. When they pulled the curtain on the Wizard (the object of their fear), they saw that what they feared had no real power and nothing of value. The Wizard had merely put on a big drama, using their fears for his power. Doesn't the Wizard sound like the Inner Critic to you?

Like the characters in *The Wizard of Oz*, we need to face our fears and see that negativity, criticism, guilt, worry, and fear have no value. And, like the Wizard, our Inner Critic does not want to be revealed. It does not want us to see the worthlessness of negativity or that our negative assumptions are false.

Like the Wizard, the ego has no real existence of its own. It depends on a false identity made out of limiting assumptions about us, and it feeds on negativity. So, you can understand that challenging these assumptions will be very threatening to the ego. However, every time you challenge a false assumption, it will begin to crumble, like the Wicked Witch when she began to melt. As your negative assumptions crumble, the real you will awaken and begin to emerge.

Negative Assumptions

The Inner Critic makes assumptions based on your wounds and old programming. Every conclusion we make is an assumption of truth, not a fact. Once we realize that most of our beliefs are assumptions, we will be free to change the assumptions that bring us pain to ones that bring us peace. Even if our new answers are also assumptions, they are useful assumptions when they empower us to create a life that brings us joy, peace, and happiness.

When you become aware of a negative belief, ask yourself if it is a fact or just an assumption. Remember that truth always brings peace, so if this belief hurts, it can't be true. However, it is my experience that most people need to gain more understanding about the nature of these beliefs before they can discredit them altogether based on this premise alone, so begin to question these beliefs and their underlying assumptions.

Where did you get that belief? Who told you it was true? Did you hear someone say it, or did you just assume it was true by the way someone treated you? For example, if a parent did everything for you, you may have mistakenly assumed they behaved that way because you aren't capable of doing things for yourself. The truth is that people do what they do because of their own needs and wounds, not because of you.

Consider the qualities of the message giver. What kind of person gave you the message—a kind person? A hateful person? A fearful person? What state of mind were they in when they did it? Were they upset?

Learn to discredit negative messages by actively remembering that people act the way they do because of their own needs and wounds, not because of you. The messages people give can only reflect the kind of person they are and their state of mind at the time, not what you are. Even if the person meant it personally, no one (including your Inner Critic) has the authority to judge you or make decisions for you about who or what you are.

Also, be sure to notice any loving or supportive messages from inside, and write them down. These messages are especially important. They will help reinforce or help develop your Inner Coach. Write down the positive messages and keep them in a place where you will not lose them. They are very valuable. These are gems of wisdom that help you feel good about yourself. Remember, every loving thought is true because it feels good, and feeling good helps you discover the truth about yourself, which leads to freedom.

Fear Is Not Useful

I have heard so-called experts talk about "healthy fear," but I have never found anything healthy about fear, even when we are in danger. While it is true that the body pumps adrenaline, giving us the extra energy to run away from danger, we don't have to be afraid to know to run—just intelligent. Most people's fear has nothing to do with being in eminent danger or the body's flight or flight reaction. Most fear is from images created in our minds about what we imagine might happen.

In times of real danger, people seldom report feeling fear. In fact, they often talk about having surreal experiences of total detachment or of time slowing down. They are usually shocked when they realize that they weren't afraid during the traumatic experience. People commonly experience fear when they hesitate to act because they don't know what to do or because they are afraid of making a mistake. Indecision is a subtle form of fear itself, which can be very painful.

After a real emergency or traumatic experience is over, people often reflect back on the event and imagine how it could have been worse. "I could have been killed!" Please notice that while this presents itself as a very dramatic realization, it is not based on reality. It is based on pure imagination. Reflections on past possibilities that did not happen only produce drama, because the event is already over. The feared possibility didn't happen and is not slated to happen in the future. That being said, it is not uncommon for a person's body to shake after the real danger is over, as it releases the effects of the trauma.

When we have lived through a real traumatic event in which we were hurt or injured—physically or emotionally—we may relive the pain of the event over and over again through images in our minds. Our Inner Critic generates fear by warning us that it will happen again. There is nothing healthy about this fear either.

Do we need to fear to avoid fire? No. We simply need education about the effects of fire. I am not afraid of fire, yet I never stick my hand over a flame. I have been educated to know that fire burns. My mother taught me the effects of fire without ever burning me or filling me with fear.

My mother also taught me that good mothers worry. That is a common belief that has been passed down for generations in many families. While mothers may worry, worry doesn't help them be better mothers. In fact, it can make a mother a source of fear and negativity, especially if she fears the worst for her child. Instead of being fearful, a mother can be a source of strength and inspiration by having faith in her children to deal with any challenge.

Worry and anxiety are just other forms of fear that are not useful or healthy. You may not be able to stop yourself from being fearful or anxious right now, but you can learn to recognize those feelings and begin to question their validity.

While it may not be the truth, we still have a reason or explanation for why we are afraid. If you identify the vulnerable feelings that are the source of your fear, you will discover your unspoken self-judgments. For example, if you are anxious and you name your vulnerable feelings, you may find that you are feeling inadequate, weak, or not good enough. That means your Inner Critic is assuming that you are inadequate, weak, and not good enough—and you believe it. If you challenge those assumptions, you may find out that they are wrong and that you are far more capable and stronger than you realize. Maybe you simply don't recognize your abilities right now. Just say, "I am willing to be wrong about these assumptions."

At first you may not be able to identity the messages themselves, but you can begin by recognizing when you are feeling fearful or negative. Recognize that the fear is not valuable or useful. This recognition is a huge step, since many (if not most) people are guided by fear.

If this step seems too difficult to understand, just take in the information and put it on a shelf in your mind. That is what I do when I don't understand something. I think all of us have an internal truth meter that recognizes truth when we hear it, but we don't always understand it, so we can't always use it immediately. When an idea feels true to me, I don't have to understand it to put it on a shelf in my mind. I have a lot of shelf space there. Every now and then, I get an insight and retrieve some great gem of wisdom that suddenly makes sense.

While this may not be a step that you can master right now, just read it and go on to the next step where you choose peace. That is where the power is anyway. You can also check out the shortcuts in the last chapter to help you.

There is no one right way to learn and grow. Just take it one step and one breath at a time. When you are feeling frustrated with the process, take a deep breath and look for another way to see your problems. Intention is everything, so you will start making progress by simply choosing peace. "I choose peace." Even just saying the phrase is powerful. The universe will support your choice, and help will come to you in ways you never dreamed possible.

The powerful samurai warriors are taught to be centered and at peace at all times. Expecting nothing, they are ready for anything. They know that fear makes us weak and inefficient. Mohammad Ali used to taunt his opponents before a fight so that they would get angry and fearful. He knew that people do not think clearly when they are angry or afraid.

I had the rare opportunity to interview a man who had escaped from a prisoner of war camp in Korea, helping two other men escape along with him. I asked him if he would mind telling me his story and if I could stop him at different points during it to ask if he had been afraid at that particular moment. He agreed to do it. I wanted to know what kinds of situations actually generated fear.

He said their jeep was hit by a roadside attack, and they were thrown out of it. I asked him if he was afraid when they got hit. He said he was not afraid, because he was busy trying to get up the hill to destroy the machine gun that was firing on them. Then he heard another machine gun fire behind him, and he saw that the enemy was on the other side of the road attacking the rest of the men. I asked him if he was afraid then and he said, "Yes, because I didn't know what to do."

He continued his story, telling me about the torture and his escape, recounting that the only times he was afraid was when he didn't know what to do. The rest of the time he was busy doing something productive in his mind, like using breathing techniques to deal with being tortured. He never doubted that he would survive. He survived because he stayed focused on his intentions.

When we are tense, angry, or afraid, our reflexes are slower, which puts us in even more danger. A muscle has to let go of the tension it is holding in one place before it can tense into a new position. If we are relaxed, we can spring into action. Fear, anxiety, or worry will not stop bad things from happening and will actually make us more vulnerable to being hurt.

Fear Is Not a Guidance System

People usually treat fear like a guidance system, avoiding anything they fear. In this misguided manner, they operate as if fear was a sign that real danger is present. They believe that they shouldn't do anything that causes them fear. Their mind says, "That's scary, so I'd better not do that, or I will get hurt." This is not true, and I can prove it.

In 2001, when the Twin Towers went down on September 11th, there were many people who were supposed to be in the towers that day but weren't, for various reasons. You may have heard some of these stories. One man's wife called and asked him to come home to help her with something. Another person was invited to a social gathering. Someone else took the day off to do some creative work. Of all the stories I heard, the one story I didn't hear was, "I just couldn't force myself to go into the towers that day. Something told me something terrible was going to happen." Did you hear that story? I didn't hear about anyone staying away because they were afraid to go into the towers. They were all guided to be someplace else.

Guidance does not use fear to guide us, because it is loving and fearless. Guidance does just what its name implies; it guides us toward something that may take us out of harm's way. Most people do not know that they even have guidance. Not following our guidance is often how we learn that we have it. Haven't you ever had a gut feeling to do something that you didn't do only to regret it later? If you always followed your feelings, you wouldn't know that there can be negative consequences to *not* following them.

Fear, worry, and anxiety are emotional reactions to an imagined future, not reality. Fear is the emotion generated when you assume that something bad is going to happen. You imagine that you will get hurt. The brain doesn't know the difference between a physical event and images in your mind, so it produces adrenaline and prepares you to defend yourself or run, regardless of the source of the images.

Fear is usually an emotional reaction to your imagination. It is not a prediction of a real event. However, if you let it, the Inner Critic can cause you to avoid taking action out of fear, which in itself could have negative consequences. The Inner Critic often warns us of danger, but if you pay attention to these warnings and follow its advice, you may avoid your own happiness.

Common Warnings

The Inner Critic often warns people to stay away from positive experiences for fear that something bad will happen. However, following the Critic's advice will often cause the event it was supposed to prevent. For example, if we follow the Inner Critic's advice to stay away from people in order to avoid getting rejected and being left out, we end up getting left out anyway. Out of the fear of a potential negative experience, you may miss out entirely on the positive aspect of an experience. The Inner Critic uses faulty logic that deprives you of happiness. These are some of the most common examples of warnings people get from their Inner Critic. The warnings are often connected to faulty logical conclusions. Remember, all conclusions are assumptions and subject to error.

Warning: If things are too good, something bad will happen.

Faulty logical conclusion: Good things cause bad things to happen.

- Therefore: There is a terrible price to pay when good things happen.
- Therefore: I have to make sacrifices when good things happen.
- Therefore: I don't deserve to be happy.
- Therefore: I am not supposed to be happy, so I get punished when good things happen.

Have you noticed that darkness always follows the light? Each day, the sun comes up, and it is always followed by the night. Wouldn't it be faulty logic to conclude that the day causes the night? It is simply part of a natural cycle. Life is full of cycles of light and darkness, highs and lows, ups and downs, and this does not mean that one causes the other.

The Inner Critic treats a natural cycle like a causal agent, resulting in you resisting life's natural ebb and flow. By learning to accept and learn from all aspects of life, we don't miss out on the joy.

Warning: Expect the worst, so you won't be disappointed, because you never get what you expect or ask for anyway.

This is a typical example of taking a shred of truth and distorting it. Scientists have noticed that nature is infinitely creative. For example, no two snowflakes are alike. While things may appear to be alike—and may in fact be similar—no two things are identical. An image in our mind never looks exactly the same way as it does when we see it in the real world. So, no matter what we expect, nothing ever turns out exactly the way we imagine it.

It is a fundamental law of physics that anything given energy will grow. Therefore, if you listen to the Inner Critic's warning, you will give energy to disappointment and lack, seeing yourself as never getting what you want. The problem here is that you will end up being right, because you have a creative mind that will create what you think about most of the time. However, if you give energy to whatever you enjoy thinking about, life will get better, because you are giving those positive thoughts energy instead.

Warning: This is too good to be true.

Faulty logical conclusion: Good things can't be true.

- Therefore: I shouldn't believe good things about myself.
- Therefore: If someone compliments me, they must want something, because no one could really think such nice things about me.

This statement assumes that only bad things can be true. When a person is depressed or suffers from low self-esteem, they assume that their depressed state is the truth about life, instead of seeing it as simply reflecting the emotions they are currently experiencing.

Warning: Avoid loving relationships, or you will get hurt.

If you follow this advice, you will end up with the pain of loneliness, without ever having had the joy of love. Like it says in Alfred Lord Tennyson's poem, "'Tis better to have loved and lost then never to have loved at all."

Warning: Avoid Pain

All of the Inner Critic's warnings are similar: avoid pain at all costs. The problem is, when you avoid pain, you are resisting it—and resistance magnifies whatever you are resisting. Resistance is the pain. Whatever we resist persists and grows. If we avoid pain, we avoid life itself with all its ups and downs, and we bring about more pain by doing so.

We simply need to be ok with our pain, and it will diminish or disappear as we begin to heal. Acceptance is the key. Just remember that the heart is open the degree to which we allow things to simply be what they are.

If you cut yourself, you have to tell the doctor where the wound is, or he can't help you. If we avoid pain, we can't heal our misperceptions. We have to be able to confront our critical thoughts about ourselves in order to discount their validity and discover the loving truth about ourselves instead.

Wouldn't it be wonderful to find out you are wrong about the beliefs that have brought and continue to bring you pain? That doesn't mean that someone else is right or wrong. It just means that the painful ideas are distortions of the truth, not the truth itself. If even part of an idea is false, it distorts the meaning of the idea. Discount the value of all negative assumptions.

Step Three: Flip It

Energy can only run in one direction at a time, so it's time to take action and change the direction of your energy from negative to positive. We need to flip it to turn the energy around. This perceptual shift will take you in the direction you want to go. However, you can't let go of anything you value until you realize it won't get you what you want, which takes the value out of it. When you want happiness and freedom, and you genuinely realize that negativity will not bring you happiness, you are able to discount it and refocus on what really has value—what you *can* do to be happy and free.

"Flip It" is the step that your Inner Critic will object to the most, so don't let it fool you. Hang in there, and read this chapter carefully. There are four kinds of negatives, and they all contain false assumptions. The first kind is just a simple negative assumption, which is easy to release, but there are three kinds of negatives that are especially hard to release: errors, offenses, and ongoing problems. Understanding how to release each of these is important, and I will cover all of them in this chapter. Making this flip is a powerful process that requires your deep understanding.

Release Negativity and Choose Peace

Now that you know (1) the source of negative feelings is in your mind; (2) your negative beliefs and judgments are assumptions and the result of your programming; and (3) you are innocent; these understandings leave you free to take action and change them. Imagine a big, round, red DELETE button in front of you, and have fun pushing it each time you recognize negativity in any form. If you have any thoughts that try to justify criticism, fear, guilt, or worry, just push DELETE and choose peace. Or simply say, "I let it go and choose peace."

Choosing to be happy or free is the same as choosing peace. It is also the same as choosing to survive in a healthy way, because negativity distorts your perception and endangers you by causing you to make faulty decisions.

Identifying any belief or message as negative is all you really need to know to discount it as invalid, which devalues it. Critical or fearful messages are not useful in finding happiness and will not set you free. It doesn't matter whether they are true or not. Don't let your Inner Critic engage you in a debate over this. Even if a negative comment "is true," it has no value because it is destructive. Push DELETE or CANCEL, and choose peace.

You may notice that I talk about change without using the word *control*, because only the ego tries to control. It does so out of fear and resistance. We really do not have any genuine control in life—just perceived control—so our attempts to control merely bring us more pain and frustration. This is why you do not want to try to control a thought in any way, including judgment of it, because you will be stuck in resistance again. Just acknowledge it, let it go, and choose peace.

When we are in a state of love and trust, we are working with the universe to naturally bring about the best for everyone. This is something that we cannot do consciously, with control. While we may not have control over circumstances in our lives, we always have a choice in how we see things, which has a major impact on our lives.

Some Inner Critics may be saying something like this, "I was loving and trusting as a child, and that is how I got here. Aren't I just opening myself up to having it happen again? That sounds dangerous."

You used your very best coping skills to get where you are right now. You did the best you could. However, now you are older, wiser, and have more skills to handle even tougher situations than you did then, especially after reading this book. So use these new coping strategies to bring yourself the happiness you have always deserved. Happiness is your birthright.

Any real suggestion for improvement has creative value. That includes acknowledgement of your strengths and how you can best use them. A criticism just finds fault and leaves you feeling bad. It is a judgment that blocks your ability to see and accept things just the way they are.

Acceptance does not mean that you approve of something. It means only that you acknowledge its existence so that you can come to terms with it as it is. Acceptance gives you clarity and expands your awareness. From a clear perception, you can change what is present. Resisting it will not bring you happiness or set you free.

What do you want to be ... ? Caring and accepting, or judgmental and critical? Open minded or close minded? Do you want to live in peace or conflict? Be creative or destructive? You have a choice. Make that choice by letting go of what you don't want—the negativity—and choosing peace instead.

Errors

You may be asking, "But what if the negativity is not an assumption? What if I made a mistake or did something terribly wrong, and there are heavy consequences? What I did is a fact and not an assumption. What do I do about my mistake or harmful behavior and the pain or damage I have caused?"

What you did may be a fact, but the judgments you made on yourself for doing it are not facts. Those self-judgments are negative assumptions, and those negative assumptions are the reason you have feelings of heavy guilty or shame. You have made self-judgments like, "I am a horrible person ... bad mother ... bad father ... weak, stupid, inadequate, not good enough, etc." Even if you are not conscious of the exact words of the judgments, you feel the emotional negativity of them just the same.

Sometimes people feel guilt or shame even when they haven't done anything wrong to themselves or others. For example, people usually feel tremendous shame when they have been the victim of a rape or other abuse, even though they were not the perpetrators. They feel diminished by the event and assume they have been changed by it to somehow become "worth-less" than they were before. They make judgments on themselves like, "I was bad, stupid, ruined … should have known better … I must have done something wrong to have attracted it, etc." Obviously, they don't deserve to be treated like this by anyone, much less by themselves.

Guilt and shame have no value to make you a better person or to prevent you from making the same mistake again. However, the knowledge you gain from the experience can do both. But if you carry around guilty feelings that weigh you down, your perception will be distorted, and you won't get the full value and so you may do it again without realizing how it happens. When you release your judgments and painful emotions, you clear up your perception so that you can learn from the experience.

I know from personal experience how difficult it can be to let go of shameful or guilty feelings, even when we haven't done anything wrong, let alone when we have erred. Guilt can haunt us and cause sleepless nights and depressing days as the Inner Critic judges us unworthy for any number of reasons.

Guilt over our human errors has historically been a special kind of negativity that has plagued humankind, because it is so difficult to eradicate. In ancient times, many cultures made sacrifices to atone for their misdeeds. Ancient Hebrew tribes symbolically placed all the sins of their people on the head of a goat and then sent the goat into the wilderness during the biblical ceremony for Yom Kipper. That is where we get the word *scapegoat* as a term for the one that bears the blame for others.

Dysfunctional families often have one family member that plays the part of the scapegoat, and the family blames that person for their problems. Quite often the family scapegoat leaves the family only to be replaced by another family member who takes the blame.

The ego or Inner Critic always looks for someone to blame for our errors to relieve the guilt. The problem with the ego's solution is that we feel bad as long as anyone is blamed. When we blame someone else for our errors, we just trade in guilt or regret for anger and maybe even a desire for revenge. This does not bring happiness. When we make a decision that causes us to make a mistake or do something wrong, there are consequences for our error. The first consequences are self-judgments, negative feelings, and regret. The other consequences are the worldly effects of our errors on others and us, like physical damage and hurt feelings.

Too often, people wrap themselves in self-loathing, guilt, and shame, assuming that they are acting responsibly by being down on themselves. However, if we are busy looking at the past with regret or guilt, we are not looking at the present consequences of our errors and what we can do about them, which is irresponsible. Energy can be focused in the past or in the present, but not both.

Giving It Over

So what if you made a 'wrong' decision? The deed is done, the error is made, and you can't change that with regret, so don't get stuck there. Your first and only responsible action is to choose peace so that you can be clearheaded enough to undo the effects of your wrong decision and straighten out this mess. This may seem impossible, and you may feel helpless to change it, so you may need to turn over the problem to a power that can undo the consequences of your wrong decision.

The same is true when we are dealing with a negative situation or unresolved conflict with someone and don't know what to do about it. You may feel helpless to do anything, but you still need to do something, because things cannot continue the way that they are. Before you can do anything, it is extremely useful to move into a state of clarity so that you will know what to do and make wise decisions that will really help you. The easiest way to get centered and stay centered is to give it over.

This is where it is very important to have a loving relationship with your Higher Power, which I call God. (Replace that word for any word that works for you.) Whether God is real or not, we need a Higher Power to believe in so that we can trust and let go of our defenses and negativity, knowing that a Higher Power is taking care of us.

A Higher Power is able to undo the consequences of our errors if we *let* It, but we have to be willing to let go and let God. God will not take anything from us without it being our choice to do so, because we have freewill. One thing I know for sure is that miracles begin to happen when we are willing to totally give our problem over to our Higher Power, letting our Higher Power take care of it.

In giving over your entire problem or your error, you are also giving over all its consequences. Give it away. Give it all away. Give it over into the transforming fire of God's unconditional love, and you will feel your life energy return so that you can use it for good in finding happiness and peace. This negative energy will be transmuted into useful energy that can be helpful to all concerned.

When I close my eyes and see myself giving over my whole situation to the Light of God, I feel the negative energy melting away and a lightness of being begins to take its place. Sometimes I have to release it layer by layer. Each layer is a judgment that keeps me out of my heart where my power lies. Releasing these layers into the Light is a wonderful transformative feeling. The more intensely negative the problem feels, the more intensely I feel the shift. If it is really big, I feel bliss as the negative energy is transmuted. As I feel myself becoming centered again, I begin to see things differently.

Give over your problems completely. Put your Higher Power in charge of the situation. If any negative feelings return, you are still trying to fix it or understand it. Let it go. You may still be valuing the pain of your regret, believing guilt is righteous from your past conditioning. Just continue releasing it until you feel peace. Give it over completely. Don't take it back. Seek peace first, and everything else will be taken care of.

If you need to do something to change the consequences of your errors, your Higher Power will give you the clarity and understanding you need to do your part. Wait for guidance. You will recognize higher guidance by the peaceful way it comes to you. Remember the good feelings you have experienced when you've had insights or revelations of truth. Truth feels good. Wait for that good feeling to know that you have clarity about the situation at hand.

Even if this process seems unnatural or strange to you, start to digest the idea, and put it on a shelf in your mind for the time being if you need to. You may want to use this later when you understand it better and feel comfortable doing it. Before the end of this book, you will find an example from my own experience, which is in a section called, "Seeking Peace is Practical."

Offenses

"What if someone has hurt you or someone you love? What if they are guilty?" you may ask. "What if what they did is so bad that it is unthinkable? How do I let that go?"

While you are not guilty of doing anything, you are still filled with judgment and negativity about what someone else did. Nothing they can do will get rid of your judgments, and you are the one who has to suffer with the pain of this negativity. Because they are your judgments, you are the only one who can free yourself of this pain.

You may even want revenge. If you get revenge, you will still carry this negativity, and it may even be compounded by your own guilt if you do something to harm anyone. It is a lose/lose proposition. No one wins in revenge. On top of that, whomever you hurt may want revenge on you in return, and this vicious cycle will continue without benefit on either end.

Simple forgiveness is the quickest and surest way to let this go, which we will talk about at length in the fourth part of this book. Forgiveness does not condone the action, but it instead frees you from the pain of carrying the action's consequences. Forgiveness is something you do for yourself, because you want to free up all the energy you are losing to this grievance.

"But I just want justice," you say. As long as there is a winner and a loser, there is no justice, so I agree that justice is important. However, the only way justice can truly be accomplished is through a win/win solution, and you can't even know what that is when you are filled with negativity. Something may need to be done, but you may need help from your Higher Power and the universe to get real justice. What you *can* do is intend it, pray for it, and ask for help to accomplish it. The universe will guide you and support this goal if you give it over to your Higher Power.

Obstacles to Peace

Just choose peace. It sounds simple, but there are many obstacles in the way of actually choosing peace. No matter how much we want peace, we may unconsciously sabotage ourselves from having it. Let's examine some of these obstacles so that we can choose it more often, arriving at our destination of peace faster.

A. Lack of Self-Awareness

You need to be aware of the problem in order to be able to choose the kind of solution you value. We can be so accustomed to pain or conflict that we stuff our emotions and don't even notice our discomfort. We may be unaware of our own emotional state. We won't desire change if we are not aware of a need for it. <u>Our feelings are never right or wrong, but painful feelings can show us where the problem is</u>.

Awareness of our emotions has value, because <u>we can't heal what we can't feel</u>. Are you aware of your feelings and emotions, or do you stuff them or deny them? Ask yourself if you like the way you feel. You may be able to justify your anger or your sadness, but do you like it? Recognize your negative feelings, and realize that you don't like feeling that way.

B. Blaming Others for How You Feel

How you feel is determined by how you see things and the assumptions you make. If you believe that people or situations have to change before you can feel good, you are playing the victim role. Even if others change for the better, you will still be a victim, because external events will still determine your state of mind and whether or not you can be happy. Don't you want to be able to be happy regardless of outer circumstances and regardless of how others act or behave? Only then can you really be free.

You can't change others, but you can change how you react to them, and forgiveness is a way of reacting that frees you from them. Remember, forgiveness is one of the shortcuts to freedom that we will discuss further in the fourth part of this book, so stay tuned.

C. Attachment to Anger or Pain

Sometimes we actually want to hang on to painful emotions and perspectives. For example, some people love their anger, and believe—either consciously or subconsciously—that they need it to protect themselves from feeling vulnerability or pain. You can't heal what you can't feel, so it is impossible to heal from a state of anger, because anger hides your vulnerable feelings.

When we are angry, we want to prove that we are right or that someone else is wrong. So we choose to keep our anger, as well as the beliefs that justify it. We don't want to see things differently, because we are afraid of being wrong, even if we are not conscious of that fear. Emotions reflect assumptions or beliefs about the way we see things. We usually want to be right about our beliefs, even if that brings us pain. This is sad, but true.

D. Fear of Peace

Sometimes we like our pain because of the benefits we derive from it. It may get us attention, sympathy, or financial support. For example, after I was successful in removing one client's phobia, she began to cry. She was afraid of what would happen to her if she got well, as she would lose her disability income and have to function independently in a world where she felt unprepared and without the skills she thought she needed. We had to deal with her fear of getting well before she could progress any further. She needed to discover more of her strengths to know that she would be all right.

We may have good reasons for keeping the pain, but we cannot get well until we discover that we harbor these blocks to peace and become willing to feel good. What blocks your peace? Discover what it is, and find another way to get what you want so that you can enjoy feeling good.

E. The Need to Be Right

Perhaps the biggest obstacle to healing is the desire to be right. In the ego world, being successful is equated with being right and survival, so we often struggle to be right. The problem is that being right inhibits progress and the process of evolving to a new level of awareness.

Developmental changes happen in quantum leaps when we let go of familiar ways of seeing things and approach life from a whole new perspective. However, we have to let go of the old way before we can see life anew. Breakthroughs in consciousness happen *after* we give up the old way of seeing things.

Say to yourself, "I don't like the way I feel, so I must be wrong about the way I am seeing this. At least, I hope I am." This disconnects you from being attached to your thoughts and emotions, while it gives you a chance to observe them instead. The subtle detachment allows you to start witnessing your thoughts and emotions, which is one of the first steps in the enlightenment process. This step can only be taken purposely and consciously. It opens you up to looking for the possibility of finding other ways to see and deal with your situation—ways that support you instead of hurting you. We will cover this in greater detail two sections from now.

Do You Want to Be Right or Happy?

Witness your thoughts and emotions. Notice when your assumptions are painful or unpleasant. Ask yourself, "Do I want to be right (about these assumptions), or do I want to be happy?" Being wrong does not mean someone else is right. It simply means that there is some distortion in the way you see it.

Be honest with yourself in answering the question. If you are honest, the answer will be that you want to be right. If not, you wouldn't be having this problem in the first place. You will find that you are choosing for conflict in some form every time you don't like the way you feel. Once you realize that, you are free to change your mind and seek peace instead. After all, you don't like the way you feel, so it is change that you really want. Isn't it? Or is it? Once you seek peace instead of conflict, you will see the world differently.

There are other versions of this question that may be more appropriate in different situations.

- Do I want peace or conflict?
- Do I want to heal my relationship, or do I want an excuse to separate?
- Do I want to be happy, or do I want to defend my beliefs and be right?
- Do I want a loving resolution, or do I want justification for my feelings?
- Do I want to clear up things with others, or do I want to have it out with them?
- Do I want to create what I want now, or do I want to get even for what I didn't get then?
- Do I want to make others agree with me, or do I want to have a good relationship with them?

We are only conscious of a fraction of the information available to us at any one moment, because our minds filter out anything that is unnecessary to reach our goal of that moment. This is very important to understand, because all goals are based on peace or conflict, and we tend to give meaning to things relative to our goals. We make assumptions to help us reach our goals, so the truth becomes whatever is useful to meet our goal.

If the Inner Critic is in charge and we think someone is guilty, we will notice everything that proves us right and be totally unaware of any evidence of their innocence. If we are in love, we do not notice our beloved's imperfections. We have all heard it said that love is blind. However, the truth of the matter is that we are blind to anything we do not want to see. Any judgment of good or bad blocks our awareness of the way things truly are. It is not love that is blind. It is judgment that blinds us.

Ask for Help to See It Differently

Letting go is easier when you ask for help from your Higher Power to see your situation differently. You can't just think your way out of this using the same intellectual reasoning that got you into this negativity in the first place. You need guidance from outside of your intellect, and the quickest and highest source resides within your heart.

Call on your Higher Power, a friend, a counselor, or therapist to show you another way to see this situation or person, and then be open to discovering new ways of seeing. Be delightfully curious to discover a truth that makes you feel good and strong. Answers can come from anywhere when you are open to receive. An open state of mind is all you need—not the answer. The answer will come by itself, spontaneously.

The quickest way to let go and see differently is through the willingness to forgive, which we will cover in the last chapter. Letting go is a skill that very few of us have developed. Letting go is the most difficult of all spiritual lessons, but if you really want to be happy, you can learn it. When you are willing to be wrong about the way you have been seeing things, life is much easier and more enjoyable.

Step Four: Replace It

Nature abhors a vacuum, so it is essential that you replace your negatives with new ideas that support your happiness by helping you take action in a positive direction. Focus on something of real value to you. I have seen people lose the value of so many wonderful insights by not replacing their negatives with ideas that give them something positive to do with their minds and bodies. I have made this mistake myself many times. We need to replace negatives with new ideas for action.

To find powerful ideas, we need to ask empowering questions from an open mind, like: "What do I want to come of this?" … and then take action to fulfill it.

Disempowering Questions

The problem is that people usually ask disempowering questions. We need to challenge not only our negative assumptions, but also the assumptions contained within the questions we ask ourselves.

The most common disempowering question is, "Why?" Why am I so messed up? Why did I do it? Why did I make that mistake? These types of questions are disempowering because they usually contain negative assumptions. They are looking for someone to blame, and no matter who gets blamed, you won't feel good or empowered to take positive action. We want answers that empower us. As most therapists know, seeking answers to "why" questions is seldom healing.

One common disempowering question is: "Why did I create this?" This question assumes:

1. You created it deliberately and are to blame.
2. What happened is bad, even though you do not know every ramification of it and how everyone will be affected by it in the long run.
3. You actually know the answer to this question.

Since your conscious mind is only a small part of your whole mind, you are probably not conscious of the real reasons for anything you do. The whole of your mind includes not only your conscious and unconscious mind, but also your Higher Self. So, perhaps this experience is happening for good reason—one of which you are not yet aware. What I mean by this is that all aspects of your whole self created this event, and that includes your Higher Self. So it must have been created for a good reason on some level, even though that reason may be outside of your conscious awareness. Set out to find the value in every experience.

Your conscious mind may well wish to reject this process of questioning assumptions as unimportant, overwhelming, and daunting, but I assure you that it is actually an empowering process. It will come to make more sense to you as you begin to notice the questions you ask yourself and how they affect you.

There is one question that sounds like it is empowering, but actually isn't, which is as follows: "What am I supposed to learn from this?" What you need to learn for your growth will not be obvious to you at first, because you need to learn it. What is obvious is only what you already know—or think you know.

For example, you may decide that what you need to learn from this situation is patience. While you may need to learn more patience, this experience has many other things to teach you that have never occurred to you before. Remember that you are the student and not the teacher. There is so much to learn from every situation, and you do not know all that is available to learn until after you have learned it. So, just ask yourself, "What have I learned from this so far?" Now *that* is an empowering question—as you answer it, you're counting your blessings.

Unfortunately, the Inner Critic often takes control of the answers to this question and concludes things like, "I have learned that you can't trust anyone." That can't be the answer. This is just another negative assumption that you need to delete. It has no value, because it does not feel good and will only bring you more pain. This thought only proves that you still have more to learn from the situation. Similar situations will probably keep happening in one way or another until you get the real lesson. The real answer will empower you, bring you peace, and reveal more of your Authentic Self to you.

This is where most of your negative beliefs come from … faulty conclusions from the Critic. But, after all, what can you expect from someone with a false identity? If you think you are something that you are not, your perception of relationships with others will be distorted. Your Critic draws faulty conclusions from your experiences and then ardently tells you to declare it as your truth. Your truth is your experience paired with your emotions—not your judgments and opinions of it, or even your positive assumptions about it.

If you still have resentment toward any situation, you haven't learned everything you need to learn from it yet. Once you get what you need to learn, you will feel gratitude for the experience without even a hint of resentment. That is why a recovered alcoholic can say, "Thank God I am an alcoholic." This person knows how much personal and spiritual growth he or she has received as the result of their recovery process. They are able to count their blessings.

This may sound impossible, and perhaps even ridiculous, but many people can attest to its truth. Practice the lessons in this book, and you will discover it for yourself.

Empowering Questions

The best way to find answers that will empower you is to ask empowering questions. The minute you ask an empowering question, your mind opens up to new ideas and new possibilities. It all starts with creating ideas that you actually enjoy.

What good do you want to come of this? Think of the enjoyable possibilities in your world that you would like to see, even if you have no idea how they could possibly happen. In fact, don't be even remotely concerned with how they will happen. Just look at the positive possibilities. Feel them as if they were real. Enjoy the feelings of those possibilities, as if they are present right now.

When we give energy to something, new ideas emerge that will make it possible. Here is a list of empowering questions that can help you to see a situation differently:

- What can I appreciate about this right now?
- What is my happiest thought about this?
- What good do I want to come of this?
- What is the best thing I can do to help others and myself right now?
- What good purpose do I want to give to this? What is it for?
- What can I do to help create the outcome I want?
- How do I want to feel, and what can I do to create that feeling right now?
- What can I learn from this that will improve my life right now?
- What can I learn from this that will help others right now?
- What can I feel good about in my life right now?

Answering any of these questions will automatically change your energy as you begin to focus on creating what you like. You will spontaneously feel much better. We are happy when we think anything we enjoy thinking. By thinking whatever you enjoy thinking, you can be happy now. You don't have to wait for your life to change to feel better. The choice is up to you. You can be happy now and continue to progress toward even more happiness.

We often repress asking empowering questions or even daring to imagine what we would like to happen, because we subconsciously believe the outcome is not possible for us. We may also be afraid to think about what we really want for fear it will make us even more dissatisfied with what we have right now. Just remember, if you can't imagine it, you can't have it, because imagination precedes manifestation. Whether you get what you want or not, if you enjoy thinking about creating it, you will feel good now, which is the goal, and you might just end up creating exactly what you want.

How you feel in this moment does not depend on your past. It depends on what you expect to happen in the future. If I told you I was going to give you a million dollars and you believed me, how would you feel? You would probably feel happy instantly. While I can't give you a million dollars, you can choose to feel happy now by having faith that life will get better, as well as by envisioning a future that you are willing to create.

PART IV:

THE ENERGY OF CONSCIOUSNESS

Energetic States

Levels of Life

There are three primary levels of life—gross form, subtle form, and formlessness or energetic. Each subtler level of life is infinitely more powerful than the grosser ones. For example, if I threw a twelve-pound rock, I could break a window with its force. At a subtler level, I could blow up the whole house by exciting the molecules of twelve pounds of plastic explosives. By working at the subtlest level and exciting the atoms of twelve pounds of mass, I could generate enough atomic energy to light a city or destroy it. It only took twelve pounds of mass for the Hiroshima bomb. While physical things may be substantial and capable of exerting great force, the greatest power is generated at the subtlest levels of life.

There are also three primary levels of human life—the physical level, the mental level, and the energetic level. These levels respectively express as the physical body, subtle thought forms, and generalized attitude or vibration. We can initiate changes in our life at any of these levels with varying degrees of ease and success.

At the gross physical level, we can use behavior modification to change our actions or behavior. We can improve our life with more exercise, eating a healthy diet, and by getting plenty of rest. These changes require effort, hard work, will power, self-discipline, and sometimes the help of others to support us in changing our habits and sticking with it. We may need constant support and many repetitions before a new behavior becomes a habit. Making changes at this level is very difficult.

However, if we believe we have a lot to gain by changing our behavior, our beliefs support the change, and we are much more motivated to change. We don't need much support from others to do what we already want to do. In fact, we may not need any support at all. As our beliefs change, our behavior changes spontaneously. This is the power of education.

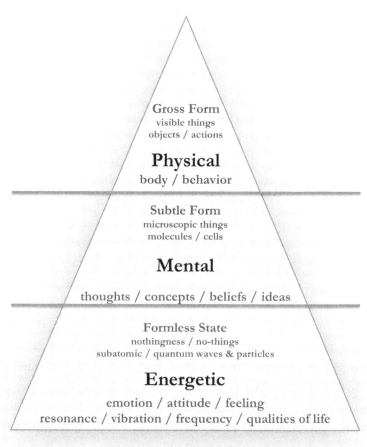

Gross Form
visible things
objects / actions

Physical

body / behavior

Subtle Form
microscopic things
molecules / cells

Mental

thoughts / concepts / beliefs / ideas

Formless State
nothingness / no-things
subatomic / quantum waves & particles

Energetic

emotion / attitude / feeling
resonance / vibration / frequency / qualities of life

Levels of Life
Subtler levels are infinitely more powerful than grosser ones.

©2008-2012 Kalie Marino

The subtlest level, our energetic state, has the largest impact of all. For example, being afraid, feeling defensive, and lacking self-confidence can make learning or any real change almost impossible, even if we are well educated, believe in what we are doing, and have the support of others. Conversely, once we make a shift to a more relaxed, open, peaceful state of mind, everything else opens up. We easily accept new ideas and behaviors, sometimes in an instant.

The most powerful life changes come about spontaneously as a result of making a positive shift in our attitude or energetic state of being. The greatest potential for power resides at the deepest level of our being, so a shift to peace is a shift to the powerful source of creative change.

In my private practice, I focus on making changes at this subtlest level, which gives me a ringside seat to miracles. This book itself is about the world behind the eyes, our thoughts, our energetic states, and ways to raise our vibrations at this level.

Raising Vibrations Changes Lives

We are energetic beings that vibrate at different frequencies at different times. We may enjoy being around some people more than others because they are loving, happy people with high vibrations. However, if you are feeling sorry for yourself, you may not want to be around happy people. You may instead choose to be around people who will agree with you and console you.

Changing our vibratory frequency changes our lives. For example, when you turn on a radio, you turn the dial to different frequencies in order to hear different stations. If you tune into a low frequency, you get a station that broadcasts on a low frequency. If you tune into a high frequency, you get a station that broadcasts on a high frequency. The same is true when you change, or fine tune, your personal frequency.

People involved in fear-based belief systems may see devils and demons, but are unable to see angels standing right in front of them, because they are in a state of fear and are vibrating at such a low frequency. If you are filled with love, it does not matter if demons really exist or not, because they do not exist at your frequency or in your world. They have no effect on you.

Raising vibrations is the goal of all self-development approaches. Whether you are moving from fearing to loving, hating to sharing, or judging to caring, any treatment or technique that raises vibrations is useful in bringing about happiness. There are many such processes.

Yoga, mindfulness, meditation, and other spiritual practices can be very effective. Two examples that I prefer are Transcendental Meditation and the Heart Rhythm Practice, because they bypass the conscious thinking mind, raising your vibrations quickly and powerfully. Inspirational music also lifts our spirits and opens the heart. I particularly like chanting, gospel, and religious music, as well as classical and new age music. Heartmath.org has wonderful tools for raising consciousness and changing vibrations, as do many sound healing teachers. *A Course in Miracles* offers a mind training practice that has changed the lives of millions of people who have read it. Thankfully, the list of consciousness raising practices is very long.

Talk therapy alone does not usually address the energetic nature of trauma, because trauma is not all in your head. It is stored in the body where energy psychology techniques can rapidly bring about miraculous changes in body and mind. EMDR, EFT, and Faster EFT are only a few of the many energy psychology techniques that are very effective in this area. They get rid of the trauma by transforming the negative energy associated with the events, helping people recover from trauma rapidly. People suffering from post-traumatic stress disorder (PTSD) make dramatic improvements using these modalities. You can read more about these approaches to wellness, plus many more, on my website at www.OpenHeartResources.com.

Another way to raise vibrations is to be immersed in powerful, high vibration energy fields of any kind, such as specially charged crystals, or crowds of loving people either singing or at prayer. You can also benefit from being around the higher vibrations of loving people. I have been blessed to spend time with and learn from some powerful spiritual teachers. They have changed my life, thus enabling me to raise my own vibrations and help others do the same. A loving environment can raise anyone's consciousness, and love itself is contagious.

Emotional Energy

Feelings Versus Emotions

All emotions are feelings, but not all feelings are emotions. The body feels the vibrations of experiences through all five senses. For example, we feel the vibrations of light waves as they hit our eyes and are then translated into images in our mind. Our ears translate the vibrations of sound waves hitting the eardrum. We feel hunger and thirst, warmth and cold, softness and hardness. Feelings are triggered by both physical stimuli and images in our mind. If we imagine eating a lemon, the feeling of it makes us salivate.

Just as the five senses gather information as vibrations and translate them into images, sounds, kinesthetic sensations, smells, and tastes, the mind gives them meaning. The mind combines the information it feels with its stored data of memories, subsequently arriving at a conclusion about what it is experiencing at any given time. It then labels the information as harmful or safe, useful or unimportant, desirable or distasteful, good or bad, etc., depending on our past experience with something similar.

These conclusions are faulty, because memories change over time. Our memories are not little packages of data that remain constant, even though each memory feels authentic. The act of remembering changes the memory itself in light of our present attitudes and knowledge, distorting the memory.[3] So, not only is our memory subject to change, but our perception of the original experience was distorted in the same way.

---

3   Jonah Lehrer, "The Forgetting Pill", Wired, March, 2012

Information and stored data come together like pistons in a car and explode upon impact, creating energy. How much energy they create depends on the amount of stored data that is ignited. This charged energy is a reaction to the stimuli, called an emotion. An emotion is therefore information plus meaning.

Perception is projection. Perception includes our emotions, as it consists of a mixture of information from the present and past and how each relates to one another. Relationships in general are emotional in nature, because they contain meaning. We give meaning to our experiences based on our emotional reaction to them. In other words, the more traumatic our past experiences were, the more our past will have a negative emotional impact on our present perception, distorting it. The opposite also has an impact. The more loving and healing our past experiences were, the more they will have a positive effect on our present perceptual clarity. This is why it is important to focus on loving and healing now, so that you have a positive outlook and perceptual clarity going forward.

Mind and body work together. For every thought, there is an emotion; for every emotion, there is a thought. Thoughts are mental images, which can be experienced as words or ideas, pictures or colors, senses or even holographic knowing. Mental images stimulate emotions and felt bodily senses. Whenever we feel an emotion or felt bodily sense, our mind is activated with thoughts of some kind, even if they aren't in words. So, being aware of our emotions and the emotions of others can give us valuable insights into our life experiences.

The belief used to exist that you had to keep your emotions under the control of your intellect. With the discovery of emotional intelligence and corresponding brain function, that idea has been discarded. Now we know that reasoning and problem solving require intuition to be able to tell what is important from what was unimportant. A tumor in the frontal lobe of the brain—where both reason and emotion are processed—can destroy a person's ability to reason and make decisions.

Being emotional does not mean that we are irrational, because emotions have logic of their own. They do make sense. We can use them to guide us and speed up our learning process by gathering information. Regulation of emotion only comes through understanding our emotions, not through suppressing them.

Emotional Vocabulary

Some of the most intelligent people with high IQs may have very little emotional intelligence, or EQ, because they are unaware of their feelings and are unable to read the emotions of others, causing problems in relationships and in job performance. EQ is a better predictor of how children will turn out than IQ in achievement test scores. However, unlike IQ, emotional intelligence can be learned. It can be improved through personal development, the acquisition and understanding of emotional vocabulary, and awareness of felt senses and body language.

Emotions are holographic energy fields. More specifically, an emotion is charged energy that contains powerful fields of information. But because this energy cannot be seen with the physical eyes, heard with the ears, or felt as solid objects by the hands, we may not place as much value on them as we do things that have substance. Emotions are a language unto themselves that many people do not read or understand, despite the fact that it is emotions that touch our hearts and motivate us to take action.

If we don't have a word to describe an emotion we are feeling, we will not notice it. We may feel uncomfortable, but we will not know the source of our discomfort, so we likely will not do anything about it. If it bothers us too much, we will think someone else is causing it, stuff it, or deny it, and stop feeling it completely. If we don't listen to this message from the body, it will eventually cause a physical problem that we can't ignore.

When children are small, we make flashcards of nouns and verbs to help them develop a vocabulary. However, there are no flashcards for the subtle emotions that we feel—a language that touches our souls and is at the heart of our humanity and all intimate relationships. The ability to recognize any specific thing comes from having a name for that thing. If emotions are not named, how do we develop an emotional vocabulary beyond angry, sad, bad, and happy?

Children are sensitive to vibrations and feel other people's emotions. If the adults who raise these children express their emotions, the children learn names for the subtle emotional vibrations, and they develop not just an emotional vocabulary, but also insight into other people and relationships. They see the interaction that goes with these emotions and how people respond to them. They also learn how to discern where emotions are coming from, instead of assuming that all of the emotions they feel are their own.

For example, if parents get a divorce, but don't talk about their feelings other than anger, the underlying vulnerable emotions are still there, unexpressed or denied. Children are sensitive to vibrations and feel the emotions without any understanding to go with them. They feel the sadness, guilt, vulnerability, betrayal, sense of failure, and anger—all of the usual emotions associated with separation—and they see their parents' sad expressions and hear their anger. Feeling all of the negative emotions without any understanding to go along with it, the child assumes these emotions are about him or her. Commonly, children assume they are to blame for the divorce and feel their parents' guilt and sense of failure as their own.

When we experience things through our five senses, we identify objects as outside of us. For example, you may look across the room and see a red ball. You've identified it, there it is, and there it stays (assuming nothing moves it). However, we can sometimes have a harder time identifying emotions. For example, if your partner is angry and doesn't tell you that he or she is angry, you will still feel the vibrations of their anger. But where would you feel this? You would feel it inside of yourself. It's not simply left where they're standing or sitting. So you would very well assume it is your anger, and your intellect would try to figure out why you feel angry. Unfortunately, most people can usually find something to justify their anger and so they get upset needlessly. The point of all this is to say that the anger you feel may not be your own.

When you feel an emotion, ask yourself, "Whose emotion is this?" It may not be yours. My first spiritual teacher told me that I was a psychic garbage pail and that I should ask where my emotions come from. This question changed my experience of the world. It is a question I still ask at times.

Unlike other information that comes through the five senses, emotions are self-created in the mind. They are unique and personal to the person creating them. Emotions generated by different people going through the same experience may be totally different, and this difference is not available through the five senses. Your emotions are personal and go on behind the eyes, where no one knows for sure what you are feeling unless you tell them or unless they have learned to accurately discern emotional energy. Sharing your emotional experience with your partner is a part of intimacy or "in-to-me-see." Sharing emotions gives you insight into each other, but you cannot communicate what you cannot name if you don't have a sufficient emotional vocabulary.

There is a lot of confusion as to what an emotion really is. For example, just because you say "I feel" does not mean that you are expressing your emotions. When you say, "I feel *that* ... ," it would be more accurate to say, "I think ... ," because you are expressing an intellectual idea, opinion, or judgment—not your emotions. When you start with, "I feel *like* ... ," you are giving an example of your emotions in the form of a metaphor, which can be very revealing, descriptive, and useful, but it is not an emotion. For example, let's take, "I feel like crying." Even though a metaphor is expressive, it does not name the emotion. Tears can express grief, sadness, or joy. These are very different emotions. An emotion is actually only one word long and is not preceded by the words *that* or *like*. Examples of emotions are sad, happy, betrayed, lonely, excited, vulnerable, etc.

Each emotion expresses a hologram of information about what is going on inside the private world behind your eyes. If your spouse tells you that he or she feels betrayed, hurt, lonely, or grateful, that one emotional word expresses more than many words could possibly say, giving you insight into your significant other.

Emotions as Objects

My deceased spouse had a unique childhood, because he was born with his third eye open and could see the energy of emotions as objects in space. His psychic vision would turn on and off, sometimes at inopportune times. When he was in the first grade, his vision turned on during class while the teacher was telling a story. He was fascinated by the beautiful pink balls of light that were popping up from each child's head as they felt affection for the teacher and the characters in the story. The balls of light, called *thoughtforms,* were floating over and sticking to the teacher's energy field, called an *aura,* until it looked like fuzzy balls of cotton candy surrounding her.

When the teacher switched to math, the thoughtforms above the children's heads became green, which represents learning and growth. Now the green balls were floating over and mixing with the pink balls around the teacher. The lights became so thick that he couldn't see the writing on the blackboard. That's when she called on him to read what she had written. He said, "I can't see, Teacher. The pretty, colored lights are in the way."

The teacher was shocked and accused him of lying, so his mother was called to school for a conference. His mother was in a difficult situation. While she supported him and his gift of vision, she knew the teacher wasn't going to understand that emotions produce light energy, so she simply said, "All I know is that Arthur never lies, and if he said he saw pretty, colored lights, then he saw pretty, colored lights."

Vulnerable Feelings

Emotions can be separated into two main categories. There are vulnerable feelings, and there is anger and its related emotions such as irritation and frustration, which mask vulnerable feelings. Vulnerable feelings are emotions we feel about ourselves relative to others, while anger is an emotion that separates us from others by blaming others or our self for how we feel. Anger does not reveal anything personal about us, nor does it reveal the vulnerable emotions that cause our anger.

Anger makes us feel stronger, so we often use it as a defense. But, make no mistake, vulnerable emotions are the reason for our anger. Intimacy is based on sharing vulnerable feelings—not hiding behind a mask or wall of anger. Anger blocks communication, because it is perceived as an attack. The recipient of the attack will automatically either shut down or defend against it. His or her heart is not open to anything you have to say as long as you are angry, so you aren't heard. If you want to be heard, or if you want to be an authentic person with rewarding intimate relationships, you will need to get in touch with your vulnerable emotions and share them.

Another problem we have with emotions rests in identifying with them as what we are, instead of just feeling emotions as the energy created by our reactions. We say things like, "I am angry," or "I am sad," instead of, "I feel anger," or "I feel sadness." If you were cut by a knife, you would say, "I feel pain." You wouldn't say, "I am pain." When we feel emotions, we don't *turn into* these emotions, as is implied by our words, "I am _____." The emotions don't change who we are. They are temporary, because they are energy we feel at that moment and not at all moments. It is useful to change how you express emotions and state your real relationship with them by saying, "I feel" instead of "I am." It helps you witness your emotions so that you can change them.

Just as we are not responsible for the thoughts that spontaneously come into our minds, we are not responsible for the emotions we feel. However, we are responsible for what we do with them. We can vent them, cling to them, or heal them and have peace instead. Your only responsibility is to choose peace. We are the only ones who can change them, and we can't do that unless we are aware of them. Awareness is always the first step to change.

Emotional Layers

In the chapter on identification, we talked about how the ego (false identity) was formed out of feedback from others and our environment. We identify with our body and other limits as what we are. We identify with our status, our roles, our money, our job, our family, etc.

Being identified with limits, we feel vulnerable and therefore insecure. We believe we can be hurt or even die, so we must be on guard to defend ourselves. We feel vulnerable to attack. Vulnerability is the underlying feeling on which the other reactive emotions are based.

In the chapter on identification, we also talked about how the foundation for these emotions comes to us through feedback from others. This feedback became our programming, which our Inner Critic repeats to us throughout our life. The basis for this underlying feeling is not the truth about us. It is what we have been programmed to believe about ourselves, and this programming hides our real identity. However, programs can be changed.

Since we feel vulnerable, we look around and compare ourselves to others, checking for their weaknesses so that we can defend ourselves. By comparison, we always come out less than others in some way, so we judge ourselves to be "not good enough," and we feel shame, which is the second layer of emotions.

The Inner Critic blames us for not being good enough, too weak, or too stupid. After all, we are the ones that let this happen. If we were just stronger, tougher, smarter, richer, etc., this never would have happened.

This self-criticism makes a layer of shame and self-doubt that can be called guilt. We feel guilty for being what we are and for not being better than we are. We feel guilty without ever doing anything wrong. We feel guilty for just being what we are. While this layer of guilt may not make sense to our intellects, we feel it anyway.

Even if we tell ourselves that we are better than others, we are comparing ourselves and competing to feel good, which gives the same defensive result. Feeling 'better than' does not feel good, because we separate and isolate in it.

We may be totally unaware of this emotional layer of self-blame. It may not have been identified because we don't notice anything we cannot name or label correctly. Self-blame is usually the last layer of emotion we identify. It is also the most liberating one to recognize.

Guilty people are afraid of being found out and punished. So, based on this layer of guilt, we have a layer of fear. We are afraid that our vulnerabilities will be discovered and we will be hurt, punished, rejected, or killed. Some people believe in a god that will punish them for not being good enough. Whether there really is a punishing god or not does not matter to the emotional body, because you can't reason with emotions. Emotions are reactions to your assumptions about the nature of reality. That being said, you are free to deny your emotions or heal them.

I know one thing for sure. I am a very loving and forgiving person, and I can't be more loving and forgiving than God. There are many people who are also loving and forgiving, and I don't think any of us would do the terrible things that people accuse God of doing. This has to be a misunderstanding. People who believe in a punishing god have a great day coming. They get to discover a loving, forgiving God.

Anger as Mask or Motivator

When animals feel cornered and helpless, they turn vicious. They snarl and try to bite anyone who comes near them. I am sure you have seen people react the same way. Sometimes emotional pain becomes so great that we feel helpless and fearful, and so we lash out at others, just like animals do. When people feel hurt, afraid, or filled with grief, their anger can become so intense that they fly into a rage. It is our fear that causes us to attack others.

layers of
vulnerable
emotions
based on
false
identity

anger/hurt
critical of others, blame others
(Blocks awareness of vulnerable feelings)

fear/concern
guarded, defensive

guilt/shame
self critical, self blame

limited/inadequate
compares self to others

false identity
based on feedback from others
and environment

©2012 Kalie Marino

Our vulnerable emotions disappear when we focus outside our self and onto the actions of others, blaming them for the way we feel. This is a powerful defense from the attacks of the Inner Critic, which is actually the biggest source of our pain. We can't get away from the Inner Critic. We can't divorce it or stop it from speaking to us, but we can ignore it by focusing on others. Anger is a way to put a lid on the Inner Critic's attacks against us. Anger is a mask that denies the vulnerable emotions we don't want to feel, like helplessness.

Because anger stuffs vulnerable feelings, it can be as addicting as any drug. Habitual anger is a dangerous form of critical addiction, because it causes things like road rage and domestic abuse. It is very important that people are educated to recognize this form of critical addiction so that it can be detected before it causes severe or life threatening consequences.

Anger can also be useful if it helps us become aware of our hurt feelings, so that we can do something about them, like get help. Sometimes people have to get angry before they will take action to change their situation. Anger makes people feel strong temporarily, and sometimes long enough to initiate change.

Anger is especially useful when a person is in a habit of blaming themselves for the actions of others or consistently taking all of the responsibility for what happens in a relationship. They may need to get angry to be able to confront others. While using anger to confront others is not the best way to handle a situation, it may be the only way a person knows how to do this. However, if you want a long-term solution for a problem, you need to be heard. And no one can hear you when you are angry, because they are typically too busy defending themselves.

When you are attacked, you put up a wall to defend yourself, and so do others when you attack them. Anger is an attack. Anger is abusive. However, if you share your vulnerable feelings, like your fears instead of your anger, you will be surprised at how receptive people become. When people feel safe, they can listen. When you express your vulnerable feelings, others can empathize with you because they have those feelings too.

Anger is attractive because anger feels more powerful than vulnerable emotions. Anger and all of its related emotions like frustration and irritation hide our vulnerable feelings and give us the illusion of strength. However, anger is not as powerful or as rewarding as joy, love, appreciation, gratitude, and caring—emotions that are not available to us as long as we are angry.

Anger is a mask that hides your vulnerable feelings. When you get angry, ask yourself what caused your anger. Are you so hurt that you got angry, or are you afraid of something? What are you afraid of? You can't heal what you can't feel, so get in touch with the vulnerable emotions that are underneath your anger, and take the necessary steps to heal them. What is your Inner Critic saying about you? Is the Critic blaming or shaming you? Use the Four Steps to Freedom found in this book to heal these emotions and negative assumptions about yourself.

Open or Closed Energy Systems

Everything is essentially energy, and energy is either creative or destructive. The energy field of any organic system either expands and embraces its environment, becoming more organized as it grows, or it contracts and separates as it decays and dies. As systems grow, they embrace and integrate. But when they resist and contract, they decay and start to die.

As humans, we are also energetic beings, and so our energy fields either embrace and integrate with our environment or contract and defend against others. We are always either open and receptive to others or closed and resistant to those around us—open minded or closed minded.

The same is true of us as individuals and groups. We are always open and embracing or closed and defensive to some degree. This is our energetic state of being. However, only open systems experience the joy of life.

Two States of Consciousness

Experientially, there are two energetic states of consciousness. Moment by moment, we are in one of these states or the other, and we can tell which state we are in by how we feel. In each moment, we either feel connected to others and the environment, or we do not. When we do not feel connected, we feel separate. It is that simple. The state we are in at any given moment determines how we see the world and whether we experience peace or conflict.

When we feel connected, we feel whole and complete. Knowing we have a lot to give, we are willing to give of ourselves and share what we have. This puts us in a high-performance state where everything works. It is like being "in the zone," having a "runner's high," or being "turned on." We have no thoughts of self in this state. We are just busy being whatever we are being—creative ... loving ... appreciative ... happy ... powerful ... strong ... focused ... joyful ... etc.

This is a dynamic state that contains the joy of life. We could call this a state of joy or state of love. Whatever we call it, this is the state that everyone wants to be in, because we enjoy life in this state.

Most people are more familiar with the other state, which is the state of separation. When we feel separate, we feel alone and vulnerable to attack. We know that the other person may not like us or may hurt us. In this state, our emotions could range anywhere from "the pit of hell" to just feeling neutral. But neutrality is not joy. We see ourselves as trying to survive in a world where we must compete for everything, whether it is love, attention, money, or things. In this state, we identify with things like our bodies, roles, social status, financial state, and other limits as the definition of what we are. In other words, we identify ourselves with our false identity or ego.

When we feel separate, we are acutely aware of ourselves. In fact, we think about ourselves constantly. We are "self-conscious." We do a kind of reflective thinking in which we attempt to look at ourselves through the eyes of others, imagining what others think of us. We do this to protect ourselves from loss, disappointment, or disapproval. In this defensive state, fear is so all-pervasive that we may not even notice we are afraid. It is as if the word *fear* is written on the wallpaper of our minds. From this state of fear, we look out on a dangerous world where we can get hurt.

Moment by moment, we are either feeling connected or feeling separate, in a state of joy or a state of fear, a state of peace or a state of conflict. There is no state that exists in between feeling connected and feeling separate.

I've already mentioned *A Course in Miracles*, which is a book about the world behind the eyes. It explains how to move from a state of fear into a state of love. This movement creates a perceptual shift in which we see the world differently. *The Course* calls this perceptual shift a miracle, because we look out on a different world from our new state of mind—a world where anything is possible.

The word *love* has been misunderstood, abused, and misused. In this book *(Breaking Free from Critical Addiction)*, I refer to love as a state of mind. We have been taught to think of love as a commodity that can be traded and exchanged, like merchandise in a business relationship. "If you love me, you would … " Many hurtful things have been done in the name of love. In reality, they were not done out of love, but out of a need to control. So the word *love* itself can engender fear of control and manipulation.

Love is actually an all-inclusive, open state of mind and heart. A bride and groom on their wedding day don't just love each other; they love everyone. We cannot be in this state with just one person without being in this state with everyone around us, at least for that moment. If you are feeling loving and appreciative of someone when you suddenly become aware of someone else you strongly dislike, what happens to your loving feelings? They either disappear, or they change the way you see the person you dislike. If your loving feelings disappear, you may still have an idea or concept of love for the first person, but you are no longer having the direct experience of feeling open and connected to them, because you have changed states. If you aren't appreciating someone, you don't love them in that moment. You can't love what you don't appreciate. However, if you manage to keep your loving state of mind instead, you will be able to appreciate the second person even though you previously disliked them. You will find something about this person to appreciate.

Love is a state that is total, like feeling connected. You either feel connected or you don't. You are either in a state of love and joy or you aren't. I think this state could be more accurately referred to as the following: "being in your love." In a state of love or joy, our energy feels radiant, like the sun that shines on everything the same.

In a state of fear, our energy could be compared to a black hole in space that is pulling in energy, because it is a state of lack in which we focus on trying to get our needs met—trying to get approval, trying to get acceptance, trying to get love, trying to get money, etc. In fear, we are focused on getting something, trying to get something, or trying to figure out why we aren't getting it. In a state of love, we are focused on giving, helping, sharing, or nurturing from a state of already having something to give.

Depending on the state we are in, the world looks very different. When we are in fear or lack, our perception is clouded. We may still have a concept of loving someone, but we are deprived of the direct experience of loving or appreciating that person in that moment. We may remember that we love them as a concept, but in a state of separation, we see them through critical eyes. Beauty is in the eyes of the beholder and reflects his or her own state of being. Some people mistakenly say that love is blind, because lovers aren't being critical of the ones they love. They are appreciating them and enjoying their life.

Characteristics of Conscious States

Did you know that there are as many neurons in the heart as there are in the brain? In fact, the heart contains its own nervous system and rules the higher mind. Have you heard the term *neurocardiology*? *Neuro* refers to the brain or nervous system. *Cardiology* refers to the heart. Neurocardiology is the study of the brain of the heart. These doctors know that the heart has a mind and nervous system of its own. It is common for people who have heart transplants to experience a personality change. This is because, in reality, they have also had a brain transplant. They are thinking with someone else's heart-mind.

The head-mind (brain in your head) works like an analog computer, which stores information and compares everything it sees with the past. It is the home of the ego. And, like the ego, it is purely reactive, giving off a warning signal if it believes the present is like the past in any way, keeping you defensive. When the head-mind is in charge, all the pulses of the body are discordant, including the heart pulse, brain waves, and hormonal pulses.

The heart-mind is the higher mind for two reasons. First, when a person is centered in the heart-mind, all of the pulses become synchronized and function harmoniously, improving health and wellbeing. Second, the heart-mind has the ability to choose instead of just reacting. When the heart gives a command to the head-mind, the head-mind reacts and does what it is told. However, when the head-mind gives a command to the heart-mind, the heart may or may not do what it says. It has a choice. To find out more about this, read the research that is available through the HeartMath Institute at their website, www.heartmath.org.

The chart on the next page, *Characteristics of Conscious States*, shows that these system states are totally different. These states are equally true for individuals and groups. We don't experience aspects from both columns at the same time. When we experience an aspect from one of these states, only aspects from that state are available to us. They all go together. Moment by moment, we are in one state or another. The items in each column are the exact opposite of the other, giving us the opposite experience of life, depending on our state. From our head-mind, which is a reactive state, we see a difficult world of pain, sacrifice, and struggle. From our heart-mind, which is an authentic state of mind, we see a world of possibilities in which we can make a difference.

Characteristics of Conscious States
These perspectives are reflected in the functioning states of
individuals, families, teams, and organizations.

Reactive Self [ego]	Authentic Self
feels separate from others	**feels connected to others**
■ Head-Mind Centered	♥ Heart-Mind Centered
LIMITED STATE	*HIGH PERFORMANCE STATE*
low vibration resonance	high vibration resonance
Based on Fear & Lower Emotions	Inspired by Vision & Caring
Driven by desire for personal safety, avoiding or destroying what is unwanted or feared.	*Guided by a higher purpose and vision, caring for the welfare of all.*
self-concerned, self-absorbed, selfish	centered, caring for others as Self
unethical, self-serving motivation	ethical, altruistic motivation
unconscious, self-conscious	conscious, other-conscious
seeks pleasure, drama & stimulation	seeks insight, creativity & intimacy
identified with past, body, roles, limits	identified with present qualities of being
closed, defensive, guarded, rigid	open, receptive, intimate, flexible
competitive, conflicted, divisive	intentional, purposeful, integral
reactive, passive/aggressive	creative, assertive
controlling/obedient, irresponsible	powerful, self-controlled, responsible
manipulative, detached, conflicted	authentic, caring, harmonious
logical, habitual, repetitive	intuitive, exploratory, questioning
suspicious, resistant,	trusting, allowing
dissecting, fault finding	seeing whole patterns, value finding
critical, demeaning, sarcastic	appreciative, supportive, empowering
judging, rejecting, comparing	discerning, accepting, understanding
secretive (withholding information)	disclosing, sharing
hoarding, grasping, hanging on	generous, releasing, changing
hopeless, sympathetic	faithful, compassionate
independent/dependent	interdependent, team player

Changing Energetic States

Many wise people have referred to being in a loving state of mind as a desirable way to live. The Christian Bible talks about the "law of love" as the great commandment, which says to love God with all our heart and soul, and to love our neighbor as our self.[4]

But how can we love when we are afraid? We can't. We may still have the concept of love in our mind and remember that we should or want to love that person, but in fact, we aren't having the direct experience of loving them when we are afraid. We aren't feeling loving. We are feeling fear. We can't love anyone or anything that we don't appreciate, and we aren't able to appreciate anything when we are afraid.

Jesus obviously understood this. He knew we are not capable of experiencing love unless we are in a state of love, so he gave a simple commandment to help us move into that state. He said seek to the kingdom of God first, and everything else will be taken care of.[5] Jesus was talking about making a perceptual shift that would expand our awareness and give us the power to accomplish so much more. *A Course in Miracles* says the only real choice available to us is to choose for heaven, which is a higher state of consciousness—a state of love and peace. In other words, seek peace first, and everything will work out just fine. Move into a higher state of functioning to improve your quality of life.

For example, if I was confused and didn't know whether to take path A or path B, I would be in a reactive state of mind; I would be in my head-mind. Whether I took path A or B, I would still be in the

---

4   Mathew 22:37-39, New American Standard Bible
5   Mathew 6:33, New American Standard Bible

same state and make similar mistakes no matter where I went. However, if I realize that I am not in my "right mind" to make a decision, I can choose to do whatever I need to do to raise my consciousness to a state of peace. When my awareness shifts, and I am at peace, I spontaneously know what to do. Perhaps path C will appear—a possibility that I could not see from my state of fear.

We Have a Choice

The most important thing to realize is that we have a choice. We can always choose to see things differently by shifting into a higher state of functioning. The world looks different from our hearts than it does from our heads. This powerful perspective is always available. There is always another way to see a difficult situation.

There is a famous picture called Rubin's vase[6], which is used in psychology to demonstrate a perceptual shift. You have probably seen it. My son, Angel, drew the one on this page. At first you just see a vase, but when you are told there is another way of seeing it, you suddenly see two people facing one another. You cannot see both views at the same time, and you wouldn't have seen the second view if you had not been willing to look for it.

We have a choice. We can always choose to see things differently when we know we have a choice. We can see any situation from our heads or our hearts, and what we see determines how we feel about it. However, we don't have a real choice if we don't know how to change states and see the situation differently.

---

6   Rubin, E. (1912). Synsoplevede Figurer, Copenhagen, Denmark, Gyldendal

Recognizing Choice

I still remember a highly intelligent female client whose husband brought her to my office because she had become too depressed to leave her house unaided. She hung her head guiltily and told me that her husband had taken her to seminars where she had learned that she was the one responsible for her negative state of mind.

By the time I saw her, she was not only depressed, but she also felt tremendous shame for being depressed in the first place. The problem was, she was taking responsibility for something she didn't know how to change. A person who has no choice cannot be held responsible for what is happening. I have seen this happen to so many people. This is an example of blaming the victim, and we often do this to ourselves. If a person has to kill to stay alive, they have a choice. It is a lousy choice, but it is a choice. They can kill and live, or they can die. If a person does not know anything else to do, they have no choice and therefore cannot be held responsible. This woman did not know how to be happy or she would have done it.

I asked her how she wanted to feel. She told me that she didn't want to be depressed. I told her that while I was sure she didn't want to be depressed, I wondered how she really did want to feel. Once more she told me all the ways she did not want to be or feel.

Depression is fairly common. Most people are depressed at different times in their lives. When we are depressed, we don't know what we want. We only know what we don't want. Depression comes from not wanting to feel what we feel, so we "de-press" our emotions and try not to feel anything. Then apathy sets in and life just doesn't seem worth living, leading to suicidal ideation and sometimes even to suicide itself. Nevertheless, even when we are depressed, we have to at least know what we want before we can begin to change it.

Many questions later, she had finally narrowed it down and said, "I don't want to be unhappy."

"Well," I inquired, "if you don't want to be unhappy, then what do you want to be?"

"Happy!" After her revelation, she sighed. Success at last! She had finally made a positive statement that expressed something she really wanted, instead of what she didn't want.

"What does happiness look like to you?" I asked.

She thought for a moment and then hung her head sadly and said, "I haven't got the faintest idea."

"Then you can't have it," I said. "You have to be able to see your goal to pursue it. Tell me, do you know what it looks like when your husband is happy?"

"Oh yes," she exclaimed, and went on to describe it.

"Then happiness will be your homework assignment," I said. "I want you to focus on happiness, and do everything you can to make your husband happy. Notice what happiness looks like on other people by seeking out happy people and happy places." She said she could do that and left my office confident that she could be successful with her homework assignment.

The next week she came in with a smile on her face. She stated proudly that she had not only made her husband happy, but she had also experienced some happiness herself.

She explained, "I learned a lot about happiness this week, but I learned something even more important. Before I came here, everyone told me I was responsible for my pain, and that only made me feel guilty. But no one told me I had a choice! Now I know I have a choice and how to choose what I want by seeking it, finding ways to create it, and giving it to others. Now I can be responsible for my own happiness." As the result of her powerful insight and her intention to be happy, she made rapid progress and was soon back at work.

Powerful Intentions

The word *intention* is misused frequently to refer to wishes or hopes. However, a real intention is an aim or goal that you have decided to make happen. It remains in the back of your mind and influences your actions, even when you aren't thinking about it.

A powerful intention is an outcome that you have accepted as certain to happen, no matter what obstacles appear in your way and regardless of your personal limitations. You aren't able to imagine any other outcome, even if you have no idea how it will happen—and even if it seems impossible to others. The intention is effortless, because you have totally accepted it as real now. Everything comes about spontaneously. You naturally move in that direction, and the universe appears to support you in your intention, because other events seem to coincidentally help you achieve it. Behind every miracle is a powerful intention. Intention is everything. It is good to be aware of your real intention in every matter.

A miracle is the result of a powerful intention. While I can't define a miracle, I am learning what they do. Among other things, a miracle creates a shift in perception that moves you from a state of fear or separation into a state of peace and connection. The whole world shifts with you, because everything looks different from this new state, and you see yourself differently too.

The following story from my life helps illustrate how this miracle process works in normal daily life. This miracle happened when I first started reading *A Course in Miracles*, and I was attempting to figure out how to apply its principles.

Anatomy of a Miracle

One bright, sunny day, I was sitting in my bedroom meditating, feeling waves of peace. All of a sudden, I heard my husband and teenage son arguing in the kitchen downstairs. A feeling of dread came over me as I suddenly realized what would happen next. They would continue to argue and then come get me to referee their fight, as I usually did. It was a familiar pattern in our family, but one I had not seen clearly until that moment. We see things more clearly from a state of inner peace.

Today, I wasn't willing to play referee. I was experiencing peace, and I wanted to keep it that way! I became defiant. The louder they fought, the harder I tried to drown them out, as I mentally chanted, "I want the Peace of God. I want the Peace of God." That was the lesson I was working on. My *Course in Miracles* lesson that day said to choose peace … and that when peace was truly all I wanted, I would get it.

I heard them starting up the steps. They were quarreling all the way. "I want the Peace of God. I want the Peace of God," I chanted, determined to keep my peace. I was new to *The Course* at the time and struggling to apply whatever it said to my current situation.

Soon, they were at my bedroom door. They pushed open the door and sat down in front of me as they continued to argue. Couldn't they see I was meditating? Didn't they know they were disturbing my peace?

By then, I had to admit I no longer had any peace to keep. I believed in our personal responsibility for the events in our lives, but I did not see how I could possibly be responsible for this quarrel, especially when all I wanted was peace! While I didn't understand how I could have possibly caused the quarrel, by that point I realized I had become part of the conflict when I began resenting their intrusion on my peace.

I was determined to deal with this situation from a state of peace. So, I made a commitment not to say one word to anyone until I was at peace within myself. "I want the peace of God. I want the peace of God," I continued to repeat in my mind, knowing now that I didn't have peace. However, I was certain in my intention that I would have peace if I kept choosing it, and I was willing to wait for peace, no matter how long it took.

A Course in Miracles claims, "Infinite patience produces immediate effects."[7] And that is exactly what happened, because suddenly, the picture in front of me shifted. Instead of seeing two people quarreling, I saw two people in total agreement, wanting the same thing from each other. Spontaneously I exclaimed, "Oh! You agree with each other!"

They both turned toward me with looks of total astonishment on their faces. "Agree?" They shouted in unison, both looking shocked, as if I had just slapped them across their faces.

"Yes!" I exclaimed with delight. "You both want love and respect, and you want it in the same way."

They turned to look at each other, and tears came into their eyes. In that moment, they knew the truth. They were both calling for love, but because they each felt a lack of love, they didn't realize that they each had what the other wanted and valued. In that moment of peace, we were all healed—together. And that is a miracle.

Miracles are perceptual shifts that lead to action, spontaneously. As I moved from the fear of losing my peace into a state of actually having peace, I saw the situation differently and spontaneously responded to what I saw through the eyes of love. I had moved my perspective from my head to my heart.

We don't know the right thing to do until we are in the right state of mind to see things as they really are. Anything that disturbs our peace also distorts our perception. Seeing things from peace, we spontaneously know what to do. When we seek peace first, everything else is taken care of effortlessly.

Seeking Peace Is Practical

We used to have an old furnace that ran steam heat to our radiators. I had to fill the boiler with water about once a month. One day, I was speaking with my mom while I filled the boiler, and I forgot what I was doing. I went off shopping with Mom and left the water turned on.

---

7   Text, T-5.VI.12, *A Course In Miracles*

When we came home that afternoon, water was spurting out from the radiators, flooding the carpet, pouring over the piano keys, and spraying the walls, furniture, and drapes. What a horrifying sight!

I was surprisingly calm as I walked to the basement and turned off the water. I was even calm when I discovered the furnace was ruined. Mom asked me how I could be so calm about this. I told her I had faith in God to take care of us. (Besides, I knew our insurance would cover everything.) It was easy to have faith under those circumstances. I felt very virtuous in my peace. I had been studying *A Course in Miracles* for a few months and was sure that I had passed the test of faith. My spiritual ego was in great shape, filled with spiritual pride.

The next day, a furnace man came to assess the damage. He confidently told me he would help me lie about the cause of the damage so that the insurance company would pay to replace cost of the furnace. Fear flooded my body as if someone had just injected a quart of adrenaline directly into my veins. "What do you mean, they might not pay?" I shrieked. "I can't tell a lie!"

He laughed and told me I had better learn how to lie real quick, unless I had about $4,000 to pay for a new furnace, plus the money to pay for the rest of the damage. He might as well have said the furnace would cost four million dollars, because this happened in the 1960s, when that was considered quite a lot of money. There was no way I could come up with that much money.

What was I going to do? It was winter, and I couldn't let my family freeze. Should I lie? I considered lying as I drove to work. Which did I value more—my integrity, or taking care of my family? That was an impossible choice to make. It was a double bind. I couldn't value my personal integrity over the welfare of others without being out of integrity, and I couldn't value physical comfort over integrity without believing that integrity has a price, therefore being out of integrity. My integrity would be lost by either choice. These are the kinds of choices that the ego shows us. It is just full of lose/lose scenarios. This was not a real choice at all. A real choice brings peace.

By the time I reached work, I was going over *The Course* in my mind, trying to figure out exactly how to apply spiritual principles to this situation. The still, small voice in my mind said, "Choose peace as your only goal, and give the whole situation to God." So, I kept repeating, "I want the Peace of God," but it didn't seem to relieve my anxiety at all. Fear was overriding everything.

When the insurance adjuster returned my call, I heard myself blurting out the truth. I couldn't help it. It was my habit. I trusted that if I was a good girl and told the truth, I would somehow be rewarded for my virtue. I soon found out that the good girl rule wasn't one the insurance adjuster used for paying claims. He told me the water damage upstairs would be covered, but he didn't think the insurance company would pay for the damage to the furnace itself. "Insurance doesn't cover household appliances," he said. He promised to call the main office in New York, get their opinion, and call me back later.

Trusting God and wanting peace didn't seem to be getting me what I wanted. That was upsetting, too. Nothing was working! But weren't things supposed to work out right if we do the right thing?

Then I realized it wasn't God that I was trusting! I had been trusting in the insurance company as my Source. Real peace is possible only when it is not dependent on external circumstances. As long as I saw the insurance company as my Source, I could only have peace if the insurance company paid my claim. That made peace extremely limited and dependent on outer circumstances.

Then I remembered an old affirmation, "God is my Source, my only Source." I wanted to totally trust God to take care of the furnace, one way or another. I reasoned that God could use the insurance company to take care of the furnace, but that wasn't the only way God could provide warmth for us. God had many avenues through which he could manifest support, even though I couldn't imagine another one at that time. I wanted to be able to trust God. However, at that moment, trust was only a thought. It was an idea of a state in which I wanted to be. I wasn't experiencing trust. I wasn't in a trusting state of mind. I didn't feel the peace of mind that comes with trust. I was terrified.

For the rest of the day, I chanted, "I want the peace of God. I want the peace of God." I was determined to experience peace before the insurance adjuster called to let me know what the insurance company would pay. I didn't want my peace to be dependent on the outcome of his call.

By late afternoon, I was much calmer, but I was not really at peace. When the adjuster called back, I prayed that he didn't have an answer yet, because I didn't have peace yet. I needed more time to reach a state of peace first. My prayer was answered when he said, "I won't know for sure until tomorrow." I was so relieved.

By late that evening, I was totally at peace and grateful to be experiencing peace without knowing whether the insurance company would pay for the furnace or not. I was at peace just knowing that God was in charge of the final outcome, and that He would take care of us one way or another. I had really given it over to God.

The next morning the insurance adjuster called to say, "The insurance company won't pay for the furnace." To my delight, I was totally at peace and accepting of this decision. I wasn't the least bit upset. By then, I knew I was safely in God's hands. That was some kind of a milestone for me. It felt wonderful.

Instead of crying or getting angry, as I would have done earlier, I calmly asked him to help me understand the basis of their decision. I only wanted to understand their decision, not to argue with it. The insurance adjuster explained, "The insurance policy does not cover malfunctioning appliances, only the damage they cause. It is up to homeowners to replace and maintain their own appliances." That made sense to me.

Then it occurred to me to ask him a new question. "Let me see if I understand this clearly. If my car ran into one of my appliances and damaged it, would the appliance I damaged be covered by my homeowners insurance?"

"Yes. In that situation, it would be covered under accidental damage," he replied.

A light bulb came on in my mind. "Well, my furnace didn't malfunction. I accidentally damaged it when I left the water turned on. My car didn't run into the furnace. My hand ran into it."

There was a long silence on the line. Then I heard the insurance adjustor say, "You're right. I didn't think of that. I'll call New York right away." The insurance company immediately agreed to pay for everything!

If I had still been depending on an insurance settlement to bring me peace, I would have panicked when the adjuster told me the company wasn't going to pay. My fear and anger would have completely clouded my mind, and I never would have even thought of that question. When I was at peace, my mind was crystal clear and receptive to guidance. I had clarity because I was at peace.

It always pays to seek peace first. From a place of peace and power within, everything else works out. That's just good old common sense at its best.

The Source you have or choose is not what matters. What does matter is feeling connected to a Higher Power that guides you and brings you peace, whether you call it God, Goddess, the Universe, etc. Again, if you need to put this on your mental shelf, then do so. But I highly suggest that you trust the process, and try it for yourself. Just like I did in the example above.

Shortcuts to Freedom

Out of all the emotions we can feel, love and gratitude have the highest vibrations on the lowest, most peaceful, frequency. When we are in our love or in our hearts, we experience an "attitude of gratitude" that is much more than words can express. It is a way of being in the world. It is a way of being in which we feel abundant, loving, and grateful for everything and everyone. The quickest way to get there is through forgiveness and appreciation, which are the two most powerful tools to peace and shortcuts to freedom from emotional pain.

We can't just decide to be in a state of love. Something has to move us there. This calls for a change of conscious states. So there has to be something we can actively do to shift our consciousness.

Appreciation Moves Us

Appreciation is the active ingredient in love. It is the verb or action we can take to become loving. We can't love what we don't appreciate. But we *can* appreciate what we don't love, and as we become more appreciative, we move into a more loving state of mind.

Appreciation is powerful. As you appreciate others, you feel more connected to them. As you feel more appreciative, you begin to feel good and appreciate yourself more. It transforms the person being appreciated and the person appreciating as well.

Appreciation, love, and gratitude are magical. They are unlike objects in the world, because the more you give them away to others, the more you have to give. You get more by giving more.

Appreciation is such an easy thing to do. Just ask yourself, "What can I appreciate right now? What can I appreciate right now about myself ... others ... where I am ... my life ... my family ... my body ... my work ... etc.?" The list is endless. Each time you find something to appreciate, your vibrations climb higher and higher.

The Attitude of Gratitude

When you appreciate what you have, you will begin to feel grateful, and when you feel grateful for all that you have, you move into a state of abundance and begin to live in an attitude of gratitude. This state of mind transforms life. With gratitude comes abundance, because we can only feel gratitude from a sense of abundance for what we have.

Grievances Block Us

The only thing stopping us from appreciating someone or anything is our grievances. Grievances are the past we hold against others and ourselves. Why are grievances such a problem?

1. Grievances are the baggage we carry around that distorts our perception, like wearing the colored glasses of our past.
2. If we seek revenge, then the other person wants to get revenge for your getting revenge, and so on, which is an endless cycle.
3. We can hold grudges, but we are the ones that have to feel the bad feelings that go along with those grudges.
4. We are the ones that suffer, while they can't even feel our bad feelings.
5. We are helpless to change others, but we can change how we see them and have peace instead of grievances.

The only way to escape our grievances is by letting them go. They have no value to our overall goal of peace and happiness, because they will block our peace and happiness. Forgive, and see the situation differently.

Forgiveness

Forgiveness is something we do for ourselves. It has nothing to do with the person who hurt us or how bad their crime was. There is nothing that is not forgivable, even if it is unspeakably bad. Forgiveness is not the act of condoning what they did or forgetting it happened. Forgiveness is releasing us from having to carry the pain of it.

Forgiveness brings about a perceptual shift in which we see the event from our heart-mind instead of our head-mind. From this perspective, we have understanding and compassion instead of judgment, which enables us to learn from the experience instead of just being bitter. However, some crimes are so monstrous that compassion seems impossible.

A Course in Miracles teaches that forgiveness is complete when we realize there is nothing to forgive. Understanding replaces grievances when we see a person's ignorance and therefore their innocence, which accompanies even the most monstrous acts of violence.

Forgiveness is not easy, because we cannot manipulate or make a perceptual shift happen with our intellect. We can't simply see things differently. Forgiveness requires an internal shift that only a Higher Power can bring about. Our job is choosing to forgive, because we have freewill, and God won't violate our freewill if we want to judge instead of forgive. God only asks for our little willingness to forgive.

When I am angry, my willingness can be very little, but my prayer is the same. I chant, "God forgive for me," and when I am able to let it in, I have a shift in perception and see it differently. I love the shift when it happens, because it feels like magic.

While many of us are learning how to empower ourselves by letting go of the victim perspective on life, sometimes it is difficult to see ourselves as anything other than unjustly treated. There appear to be real villains and victims in the world, and certain things seem unforgivable. Can we forgive people for committing murder and other atrocities without being in denial?

I met a woman who demonstrated we can forgive anyone for anything and empower ourselves by doing so. Through forgiveness, she transformed a tragedy of immense proportion into a lesson on love.

Forgiveness Transforms Tragedy

A friend, whom I shall call Mary, first joined our *A Course in Miracles* study group when she was going through a horrendous child-custody battle with her husband. He was severely disturbed and had projected his guilt on Mary by trying to make her think that she was insane. He kicked her out of their home and vowed that he would never give her one cent or return any of her things. He also vowed never to let her see her son, Benji, again.

He was a sick and bitter man who lived in the woods to avoid the people he hated. He taught Benji to say things like, "People are pigs." He was wealthy enough to wage a prolonged court battle against Mary, in an attempt to prove that she was an insane and incompetent mother. He hired three lawyers, two psychiatrists, and two psychologists to prove his case. After two and a half painful years, the court reached its decision. They awarded Mary custody of Benji, along with a relatively small financial settlement. He was given visitation rights, even though the judge and his own psychiatrists saw him as harmful to himself and others when he didn't get what he wanted.

He was furious and carefully set out to plan his revenge. He gave away his most valuable possessions, sold all of his stocks and bonds, withdrew his money from the bank, and took the cash home with him. Then he picked up Benji for the weekend, giving Mary a large check drawn on a bank account that he had just emptied. Next, he took Benji into his house and fatally shot him, set his house on fire, and then shot himself.

He must have wanted to make sure that the house and everything in it burned to the ground, because he cut the neighbor's telephone lines, preventing them from calling the fire department. Then he parked his truck in the entrance to his land so that no one could get up the driveway. We can only assume that he wanted to be sure nothing was left for Mary. His final touch of vengeance was that he did this horrible crime early in the morning on Mother's Day.

The initial shock almost killed Mary with grief. Then she realized that, while she couldn't change what had happened, she could choose what she wanted to come of this tragedy. She asked, "Do I want to live or die?" To her, this meant, "Do I want to continue to be myself and love life, or do I want to die a slow death through hatred of this man who murdered my son and tried to take everything from me?" Life or death; love or hate. She had no illusions about the choice she was making, for she knew that hate would block her from fully expressing her love for Benji and for life itself. Love and hate cannot coexist. To experience one is to give up the other. When we hate, we do not love.

Mary wanted to continue loving Benji and to express her love for Benji in the activities of her life. So, instead of hanging on to her grievances and infecting herself with the same hatred that had caused both deaths, Mary chose to see it differently and forgive her husband with God's help.

While Mary knew better than anyone just how cruel her husband's actions could be, she was also aware of what went on inside of his mind to cause such hatred. He was a hurt person, so he thought that by hurting others he could somehow relieve his own pain and guilt. We all do that when we choose to hang on to a grievance. But every time he hurt someone else, it only increased his guilt, escalating into madness. He couldn't face his own guilt, and so he wasn't able to forgive himself. He didn't know how to forgive, so he never released his pain. When Mary asked him why he did these things, he replied, "Because I need help."

He suffered from such hatred that he tried to take everything away from Mary, and what he couldn't take away, he destroyed, even when it meant destroying what he loved the most, which was his own son, Benji. To hate this man or anyone is to become infected with the same disease that led to his death. Mary saw hatred as a disease, and she refused to let this sickness infect her. She chose to remain healthy and loving. She didn't allow this sick man to decide how she was to live her life. She was free to love and therefore to live, which is what his True

Self really wanted for her, for that is what he truly wanted for himself but didn't know how to get.

She didn't do this alone. She has a deep and abiding love of God that she called upon to forgive her husband for her. It was the strength of God in her that made forgiveness possible and still shines as a light of inspiration for us all. She truly qualifies as a teacher of forgiveness.

Mary told me, "You can't hurt good. The devil can't penetrate God, and I want to be proof of that. I'm not going to let this illness put a piece of anger in my heart where I would have to live with it."

Mary is proof that we can forgive anyone for anything, because it is natural to love and, therefore, absolutely necessary to forgive. Forgiveness is not a luxury reserved for saints. If we are to love at all, forgiveness is a necessity. When we are holding a grievance against anyone, we are not free to be ourselves; we are not free to live, love, and enjoy life. If Mary can forgive this man, is there anyone or anything you can't forgive?

It's is okay to be angry. Forgiveness is a process that is not done alone. It starts with recognizing your resentment or anger. That's how you know there is something to forgive. Accept it, express it, and then ask God to help you release it. Let God forgive for you. Don't try to do it alone.

Above all else, don't make yourself wrong for being angry or upset— and don't fear your emotions, because your fear will make you sick. This man's fear of his emotions stopped him from seeing the real problem, which was his own emotional state. If he had been able to recognize and heal his anger, this tragedy would never have happened.

If this man had known how to make his life turn out loving and happy, he would have done it. He simply didn't know how. This is true of anyone who ever hurt you. Within their ignorance is their innocence. This is true for all of us. Within our ignorance is our innocence.

Don't think Mary didn't grieve for her son, because she did. She felt the loss of her son's touch very deeply, but she knew that the most she could do for him was to love him. At first, she struggled with how to love her son and make contact with him in a meaningful way, without the ability to see or touch him. She had to learn a new way of loving.

There is one thing of which I am certain, and I know Mary is too—her son is just fine. Like all of us, he came into this life to learn and teach love, for that is what he is and what we all are. He did a fine job of it, for in less than four short years he won the hearts of many people, while loving passionately in the middle of a war zone. What an accomplishment!

When I think of Benji, I will forever think of the power of forgiveness and miracles, for I saw a tragedy of great proportion turned into a lesson on love. Many lives in Mary's community were transformed. She showed people a new way of living ... a way of forgiving. We saw for ourselves that there is no order of difficulty in miracles, and there is nothing that cannot be forgiven.

> "Forgiveness is the key to happiness. Here is the answer to your search for peace. Here is the key to meaning in a world that seems to make no sense. Here is the way to safety in apparent dangers that appear to threaten you at every turn, and bring uncertainty to all your hopes of ever finding quietness and peace."[8]

Peace As a Social Value

Is it realistic to believe that our society can become peaceful? One of the common assumptions about the human race is that we are a warlike species and therefore only the strongest will survive. However, recent archeological evidence of our oldest civilizations suggests that warfare is unnatural to the human race, becoming a habit only during the last 5,000-year cycle of civilization.

In Greg Braden's book, *Deep Truth*, he reveals that archeologists have discovered civilizations dating back 10,0000 years. They learned that warfare has only been a part of our behavior during the last 5,000 years.[9] Previously, war was unknown. The lack of weapons, mass graves, and protective walls in the excavations of the oldest civilizations implies that they were not warlike. Survival in the earliest civilizations depended on helping each other and living cooperatively. Researchers also found four-story buildings and water reservoirs indicating that these ancestors were more advanced than was assumed.[10] This gives us a radically new picture of our past, as well as new possibilities for our future.

The theory of "survival of the fittest" is a concept that has been used to justify competition and capitalism, but it is not based in fact. "Survival of the fittest" is an economic theory first introduced by Herbert Spencer in which he drew parallels to Darwin's theory of natural selection, a theory that has been discredited by many scientists. "Survival of the fittest" is a way of thinking and living that perpetuates

---

9   Gregg Braden, *Deep Truth: Igniting the Memory of Our Origin, History, Destiny, and Fate,* Hay House, Inc. 2011, p. 186

10   Gregg Braden, *Deep Truth: Igniting the Memory of Our Origin, History, Destiny, and Fate,* Hay House, Inc. 2011, p. 190

criticism, competition, and warfare. It is a way of thinking and not a fact at all.

In part two of this book, we showed how behavior is based on subtler levels of life, which include thinking, beliefs, and attitudes. Change the thinking, and the behavior disappears, because it is natural to love and connect—not to compete. For this to change, education is essential.

Now we know that both war and criticism are learned behaviors. Children are not born critical, and the human race was not created warlike. What happened to us? While we may never know the answer to that question, we are capable of learning a new way of living together that is natural, spontaneous, and joyful.

Many people in our society are beginning to value peace as we take more personal responsibility for creating peace within ourselves. Each and every day, new methods of stress reduction become popular, and more people incorporate them into life. Not only are we learning to relieve stress in the body through meditation, exercise, and diet, but we are also learning how to change the way we see the world, so we don't get so stressed in the first place. Prevention is preferable to cure. Why should we wait until we are in pain before we seek peace?

One of the most astounding discoveries is that blissful, altered states of awareness, commonly thought to be available only through deep states of meditation, are actually available to us while we are in the midst of activity and fully participating in the world. The common experience of a runner's high is only one example of the bliss that can be found in any high performance state. The practice of mindfulness, introduced to the West by Buddhist monks, demonstrates that we can have bliss as part of our daily life by bringing our awareness into the present moment and living in a fully present way. Pure presence is pure bliss. The past and future only exist in our minds. The present moment is the only place where God is.

However, purification is necessary first to release the blocks to peaceful awareness. Purification is the sorting out process. The way out of hell is through discernment, which includes sorting out "what is" from "what isn't," truth from lies, and reality from illusions. That is the purpose of this book.

Whether we go inside or outside for our happiness, the greatest happiness is found in the present moment, in being fully aware of "what is." We can transcend hell temporarily in present moments of joy, and we can begin our inner work to dispel illusions and establish a peaceful state of mind.

The Law of Reciprocity

There is a spiritual principle that says giving and receiving are one in truth, which is actually the law of reciprocity that repeats on all levels of life. We end up experiencing whatever we give out or extend to others. This principle goes by various names. It is called karma in the East. The Bible says, "A man reaps what he sows."[11]

Reciprocity means that you receive positive or negative results depending on what you sow. So if you treat others badly, the cost of giving is receiving, which can hurt you or make you sick. I call that *instant karma*. The negativity from this is how we feed the Inner Critic.

Knowing this rule, wise people of all religions made laws and gave guidance to protect their people from the negative consequences of their own actions. Jesus said, "Do not judge so that you will not be judged."[12]

The Ethic of Reciprocity, also known as the Golden Rule, appears in different forms in just about each (if not every) religion in the world. They all seem to agree on how one person should treat another: you should treat others the way you want to be treated, because you always feel the reverberation of your actions. What goes around does indeed come back around, as the old saying goes.

When my husband's three children first came to live with us, they fought a lot and were defiant of rules. I informed them that there was

---

11 Galatians 6:7, *New American Standard Bible*
12 Matthew 7:1, *New American Standard Bible*

only one rule in our home, and it was the Golden Rule, which states, "Treat others the way you want them to treat you."[13] They could understand this rule. It made complete sense to them. In fact, they loved it. I would frequently see one of them shaking their finger at the other, saying, "Golden Rule!" They never objected to being reminded of the rule, because that meant that they could correct their own actions. It also put us on equal footing with them. We had to follow the Golden Rule as well, or they would remind us to do so. It stopped the fighting between them, and it helped us all live happier lives.

I made copies of the Golden Rule with different pictures and sent them home with couples and families, whether they were religious or not, because it is a universal ethic. Every family invariably made positive changes using this rule. Their children initiated many of the changes when they pointed out their parents' behaviors needed to change. We all know when we are being treated kindly. We just need to apply the same understanding and consideration to our own behavior.

Children love the Golden Rule. It gives them a principle to live by that solves many of their problems. Children need structure and guidelines. The Golden Rule can solve many of our social problems as well. It is natural for us to live in cooperation and unnatural to live in competition. Cooperation brings harmonic resonance and creativity.

Treat others the way you want to be treated.

---

13   Luke 6:31, *New American Standard Bible*

Kalie Marino

What would our society be like if we actually lived by the Golden Rule? Could we make positive changes in our world if we posted this rule in schools, businesses, and at home? Would families, teachers, classmates, and friends be kinder? Would workers treat each other differently if kindness became the politically correct thing to do?

Apply the Golden Rule to your life, and see how your life changes. Demonstrate what you believe. Let's live it, not just talk about it.

The Universal Ethic of The Golden Rule

Christianity	Judge not, that ye be not judged. (Mathew 7:1) Treat others the same way you want them to treat you. Luke 6:31
Native American Spirituality	Humankind has not woven the web of life. We are but one thread within it. Whatever we do to the web, we do to ourselves. (Chief Seattle) Respect for all life is the foundation. The Great Law of Peace
Judaism	What is hateful to you, do not do to your fellowman. This is the entire Law; all the rest is commentary. (Talmud, Shabbat 3id) "...thou shalt love thy neighbor as thyself." Leviticus 19:18
Islam	No one of you is a believer until he desires for his brother that which he desires for himself. Sunnah
Buddhism	Hurt not others in ways that you yourself would find hurtful. Udana-Varga 5,1
Hinduism	This is the sum of duty; do naught onto others what you would not have them do unto you. Mahabharata 5,1517
Taoism	Regard your neighbor's gain as your gain, and your neighbor's loss as your own loss. Tai Shang Kan Yin P'ien
Confucianism	Do not do to others what you would not like yourself. Then there will be no resentment against you, either in the family or in the state. Analects 12:2
Zoroastrianism	That nature alone is good which refrains from doing to another whatsoever is not good for itself. Dadisten-I-dinik, 94,5
Baha'i Faith	Lay not on any soul a load that you would not wish to be laid upon you, and desire not for anyone the things you would not desire for yourself....Ascribe not to any soul that which thou wouldst not have ascribed to thee, and say not that which thou doest not...Blessed is he who preferreth his brother before himself. Baha'u'llah, Gleanings, LXVI:8

Let's Live It!

Experiential knowledge is far different than intellectual knowledge. The wisdom of our experience resonates with authenticity throughout the universe, profoundly changing our lives and affecting people that we may never meet. Rupert Sheldrake and his theory of formative causation and morphic resonance has scientifically demonstrated time and again that experiential knowledge is made available to the entire species. What we learn through experience is added to our collective consciousness. Real knowledge is structured in consciousness. I will be talking about this in my next book on conscious creation.

There is so much spiritual knowledge on our planet—knowledge that we don't apply. We don't always nurture it and let it grow into wisdom by using it. Let's not just talk about it or read about it. Let's live it!

Perhaps more people would live it if we had a place to share our experiences, listen to other people's experiences, and ask questions about how to live it with people who care. I would enjoy being part of an online spiritual community of people who are living it, or at least attempting to live it, and I want to encourage others to do the same.

I have shared my experiences with you. Now I would enjoy hearing your experiences. Will you share your experiences with me? How have you applied the Four Steps to Freedom? What happened when you used them? Which ones were the most meaningful to you? What have you learned from your experiences?

Share your experiences and questions at CriticalAddiction.com. The stories or experiences you share may inspire others. Your questions will be questions that others have as well, so don't be afraid to ask.

There are as many techniques and ways to peace as there are people. We learn from each other and then create our own way of doing things. I want to learn from you while you learn from me.

Let's experiment with living the Golden Rule. See what happens if you post a sign like this in your home or workplace. Get people talking about it. See if they are willing to commit to using it with each other.

Then share what happens on our website. I hope you will have many other good ideas to share.

I look forward to connecting with you in the future, perhaps in person or on the web. In the meantime ... Let's Live It!

Afterword

I am sad to announce that just as this book was going to press, our son, Michael Marino, Jr., was handcuffed and fatally shot by police officers. He had committed no crime, had no weapon, and was killed in a secluded place where he was not endangering anyone. That was seven weeks ago, and my husband and I still have not heard any explanation for this terrible act. The police department and the District Attorney's office remain silent.

There was standing room only at his memorial service with over 300 people inside the building and more standing outside. Most were friends of Michael, and they told stories of all the wonderful things he had done to help others. A friend who had just returned from Afghanistan said that Michael sent a care package, not just to him, but to his whole unit every month. That's the kind of person he was. He was a kind and loving person to everyone. His friends are petitioning for justice for Michael.

Our son and the officer who shot him both suffered from undiagnosed critical addiction, which manifested in different ways in each of their lives. His death points out the importance of identifying this problem and taking action to change it. Successful treatment could have saved two lives in this case, because the officer was also damaged by Michael's death. He has to live with the consequences of taking an innocent life. I am determined to find people who are willing to join with us in identifying this problem and educating the public with ways to break free from this addiction that can be life threatening.

I am grateful for the life experiences that have prepared me for this as well as anyone can be prepared for the unthinkable. In part four of this book, I told a true-life story called "Forgiveness Transforms Tragedy" in which Mary demonstrated the lessons that can be learned from such an event. Little did I know that I was being prepared for dealing with the murder of my own child in years to come.

We have experienced a full spectrum of emotions in dealing with this tragedy, but we are amazed at the inner strength God has given us. We are okay, and we know that our son is safely Home in God. I am sure that there will be a lot more to deal with in connection with this tragedy. However, we are determined to go forward with compassion and forgiveness as we seek justice to prevent this from happening to others.

The Four Steps to Freedom and the shortcuts that I shared in this book are a habit and way of life for us. As a result, we are able to use them to work through our shock, anger, and grief to live in the attitude of gratitude even in the midst of this tragedy. The steps work. It is my prayer that they will become a new habit for many others. They remind me that we are sustained by the Love of God, who is our only Source.

Internet Resources

CriticalAddiction.com
BreakingFreeFromCriticalAddiction.com
GaryThink.com
HeartMath.org
OpenHeartResources.com
Psych-K.com

Bibliography

American Bible Society (1995), *New American Standard Bible,* New York, NY

Blakeslee, Sandra, "Mirror Neurons: Cells that Read Minds", New York Times, January 10, 2006

Gregg Braden, *Deep Truth: Igniting the Memory of Our Origin, History, Destiny, and Fate,* Hay House, Inc. 2011

Foundation for Inner Peace. (1975). *A Course In Miracles.* Glen Ellen, CA

Lehrer, Jonah, "The Forgetting Pill", Wired, March, 2012

Rubin, E. (1915). *Synsoplevede Figurer.* Copenhagen:, Denmark, Gyldendal

About the Author

Kalie Marino, MSW, is a clinical social worker, ordained interfaith minister, spiritual coach, respected leader in the field of personal growth, and popular public speaker. An expert on relationships, spirituality, and transformation, she reaches people with her positive message about personal power, love, and conscious states of mind.

Kalie was blessed to travel and study with some of the world's greatest spiritual and transformational teachers as well as quantum physics theorists throughout the world. She has led seminars all over the country integrating these subjects. Her unusual background in quantum physics, psychology, and spirituality makes her uniquely qualified to share a practical perspective on creating personal and social transformation.

People use words like *profound* and *insightful* when they attend Kalie's seminars. However, Kalie says, "I don't tell people anything they don't intuitively already know through their experience. I just help them notice the self-evident truths that they have experienced and put a frame of reference around all of it, making this knowledge useful to create happiness."

Kalie's focus has always been tailored to reach beyond the intellect to how people create authentic change and energetic shifts in perception. She researched the cause of transformational change for her master's thesis, integrating quantum physics with metaphysics and the human systems theory. Her research demonstrating that a person's state of mind can even cause significant physical effects made headlines in *The Brain/Mind Bulletin*, a national scientific publication.

You may have seen her articles in *New Visions Magazine* and *Miracles Magazine*. She has led seminars based on spiritual principles found in the book *A Course in Miracles* since 1978, and she has taught a variety of transformational processes all across the nation since 1967.

In 1997, she founded the Open Heart Institute for teaching holistic and spiritual counseling, which included numerous energy psychology techniques, which are breakthrough therapies for overcoming anxiety, stress, and trauma.

Treat yourself to a session with Kalie, and learn what is right with you instead of what's wrong with you. She is available for private sessions by phone, on Skype, and in her office in Warminster, PA. To make an appointment, call 215-672-1599, or go to her website at www.OpenHeartResources.com.